I0616379

A LINE RUNS THROUGH IT

A Wood Dragon Book

A LINE
RUNS
THROUGH
IT

A Story of Sexual Abuse,
Addiction, and Redemption

NIALL SCHOFIELD

A Wood Dragon Book

Title: A Line Runs Through It
A Story of Sexual Abuse, Addiction, and Redemption
Copyright © 2025 Niall Schofield

This book is a non-fiction memoir. It reflects the author's present recollections of experiences over a period of years.
All rights reserved. With the exception of brief quotations in book reviews, no part of this publication may be reproduced in any form whatsoever without the permission of the publisher or author. No part of this book may be used or reproduced in any manner for the purpose of training artificial intelligence technologies or systems.

978-1-990863-88-2   Audiobook
978-1-990863-87-5   eBook
978-1-990863-86-8   Paperback
978-1-990863-85-1   Hardcover

Cover Design: Yago Domingues
Interior Design: Christine Lee

Published by:
Wood Dragon Books
Post Office Box 429
Mossbank, Saskatchewan, Canada S0H3G0
www.wooddragonbooks.com
To contact the publisher: wooddragonbooks@gmail.com

To contact the author: (639) 470-7441
For more information about the book:
https://linktr.ee/Niall.Schofield

DEDICATION

To my mother, who passed away before the completion of this book.

To my mentor and good friend, Kerry Girling, who inspired millions of youth through his amazing efforts to create positive change.

To the people who may be holding this books in their hands, searching for ways to work through trauma and face their fears.

CONTENTS

INTRODUCTION

I could feel myself slipping through the cracks of life. I desperately fought to point my life in a positive direction, but my grip on reality was loosening.

Thanks to periodic odd jobs, I was swinging wildly from being able to afford drugs to missing payment dates to my dealer.. I started doing shady deals to acquire drugs that I could distribute myself on the streets of Saskatoon. I just needed to make enough money so I could keep myself supplied with my drug of choice – cocaine. For a while, my strategy worked, but eventually, thanks to my drug-infected brain operating in a state of paranoia and fear, I lost control over my cocaine business dealings. My dealer became very angry and showed no compassion for my situation.

I wasn't alone in the cocaine business in Saskatoon. There were players bigger and in deeper than I was — like my friend, Larry, who was not only moving cocaine, but was dealing in weapons as well. The more we hung out together, the more I sensed I was in way over my head. Although we were friends, listening to Larry talk about the individuals he was surrounded by intimidated me and made me wary. Some days his brash talk would falter and paranoia would take over; he was becoming more and more distrustful. He always had his guns in his truck — locked and loaded in case a business deal went sideways.

I was getting deeper involved in things I should have been walking away from, not walking towards. Desperate for help with my aggressive dealer, my paranoid, illogical brain told me to call Larry and ask for help.

Shortly after I made that call, Larry asked me to take a drive with him. We headed out of the city, each snorting coke to feed our inner demons. Soon we were driving on a deserted gravel road.

Suddenly, Larry stopped the truck and asked me to get out. I climbed out of the truck and found myself standing on the edge of a ditch. As I turned around to face Larry, I found myself staring at the barrel of a gun pointed straight at me. Larry's composure was steady. I knew how this was going to play out. I was in big trouble. The gun was loaded and the hammer cocked.

I did not flinch. I did not beg. I did not speak. I just stood there in front of Larry and his loaded gun. His eyes were glassy from the cocaine surging through his body and I could see his left eye twitch nervously. Beads of sweat were forming on his brow and dripping down his left cheek.

I silently began bracing for the impact of the shotgun blast. I froze as his finger moved off the trigger. I could see his chest expand as he inhaled. Suddenly a barrage of profanities colored the air and the barrel of the gun lowered. "Get the fuck in the truck," he said. He told me that he had been ordered to kill me, but he had decided not to. All the way back to the city he kept muttering, "You are so fucking lucky, Niall. You are so fucking lucky."

He would not say who had given him the order to kill me. To this day I do not know who it was.

This near-death incident caused me to wake up and look hard at my sorry life through a whole new lens. For the past two years, I had been living in fear of the voices in my head. My mind had brimmed with dark, evil thoughts of anger, hatred, and shame. I was drowning in fear. Steel chains bound my soul. The harder I fought, the more the darkness around me intensified.

And now I had faced a near-death experience. *How did I get here? Rock bottom. Thirty-seven years old.*

1

TONTO

I was born in 1978 in Saskatoon, Saskatchewan. Métis, with family originating from Saddle Lake Cree Nation in Alberta, I was part of the infamous Sixties' Scoop where between approximately 1951 and 1984, an estimated 20,000 First Nations, Métis and Inuit infants and children were taken from their families by child welfare authorities and placed for adoption in mostly non-Indigenous households. I was four months old when I was taken and put up for adoption.

A loving couple from Saskatoon, Bill and Sandra Schofield, adopted me when I was six months. My new parents already had three children. The oldest was Cyril. Next was Amber. The youngest was Nola. After having Nola, my mom decided she wanted another child. She suggested to my dad that they adopt. After being approved by the adoption services in Saskatoon, they began looking through photo books of babies.

The child they adopted was me.

As my mom tells it, they turned the page in the book, spotted my picture and their decision was made. She said, "I just knew he was the one I wanted." I often ask her why she chose me and she always replied, "I just knew you were special."

In due time, my parents received a phone call from the adoption agency. They could come and see me and decide if they wanted to move forward with the adoption. My mom often tells me how excited they were that day as they sat in the waiting room at the adoption office. She was finally going to get to see that little brown-eyed boy who was as "cute as a button." When the nurse brought me into the waiting room, I was dressed in a little jumper with a hat on my head.

When she tells this story, a warm loving smile always comes to my mom's face. She says that was the moment when a feeling of joy came to her heart and she knew I was the one. I am blessed to have been adopted by such wonderful parents. I had a wonderful early childhood with the Schofield family.

Andre was my first childhood friend. He had a toy garage. It had a blue roundabout ramp, a gas station, and a mechanics shop. It came with a little plastic car with four wheels that turned and a little man in the driver's seat. We would take turns using the car lift to raise the car to the upper level of the garage. Another of Andre's toys was a big red barn with chickens, cows, horses, and even a cat. There were sections of white fence that we would join together to make a fenced area so the animals could not get out. We would play with this barn and its animals for hours.

Andre had a record that he liked to listen to. It wasn't an Elvis Presley record, nor was it the Beatles. As this record played, Andre would run around the house yelling, "Hi-Ho Silver! Away!" One day as the record played on, we discovered a second character in the storyline. This second character was a side-kick to the character who yelled, "Hi-Ho Silver! Away!" His name was Tonto. If you have not guessed, I am talking about the Lone Ranger, the man with the white horse who wore the black mask over his eyes just like Zorro. Soon we found ourselves running around the house yelling. Andre was the Lone Ranger and I was the sidekick, Tonto.

I can vividly remember one day asking Andre if I could be the Lone Ranger and if he could be Tonto. I still remember the priceless look on his face. Here I was, a darker-skinned boy asking to play the role of a white man! Andre's reply to me was quite clear. "No," he

4

said, "You're an Injun. You play Tonto. He's brown like you." This sounded logical to me. On the cover of the record album, Tonto was depicted as darker-skinned. There was no hostility behind Andre's suggestion that I was an "Injun." I do, though, remember a feeling of separation and difference. My skin colour somehow influenced his view of me and he wanted me to play a specific role.

This was only the first of many similar experiences as I grew up in this white family, in a neighbourhood of white neighbours. My different skin colour was also apparent in the church community that our family was involved with. We attended the First Mennonite Church located at Queen and 25th Street in Saskatoon. Special attention was always paid to me by the older generations at church. They would greet the rest of the family with a simple hello, but wonder aloud at my role in the family. My parents would explain that I was adopted.

I have memories of all of us kids dressing in our Sunday clothes, my sisters in nice dresses and my brother and I in dress pants and dress shirts—or sweaters or vests with dress shirts underneath. My favorite outfit was a suit with light brown dress pants and a matching vest. Under the vest, I wore a white dress shirt. I felt sharply dressed when I wore it. It is funny to think of seven people getting ready for church at the same time. Girls running up and down the stairs while they looked for their tights, boys finding missing shoes or a tie that they had planned on wearing on that particular Sunday. I remember how my dad shaved in the bathroom mirror as my mom patiently waited to put on her makeup and make final touches to her hair.

I have pleasant memories of attending Sunday school with Andre. Each week, we rehearsed scripture from the Bible and did crafts such as colouring a picture of Noah's Ark. We learned about the Ten Commandments. Sunday School taught me values like, "Treat others as you want to be treated." I tried to apply what I learned in Sunday school to my everyday life even if I did not understand what it all meant.

Our after-church family tradition involved going to the Bonanza steakhouse for lunch. We typically went with Andre's family. It was always a treat. When we got home, everyone put their Sunday clothes away and carried on with the normal week of school and activities.

Andre and I often played at each other's homes. Our parents had bought us straw horses to play with. One day, Andre's father made a Lone Ranger mask out of an old cereal box. After cutting out the eyeholes, he coloured it black and attached a string to hold it in place. Andre handed the mask to me and said, "Here Niall, you can be the Lone Ranger, and I will be Tonto." Away we went, yelling and play-acting out the storyline as the record played. It was at that moment, when he handed me the Lone Ranger mask, that I knew he was my best friend.

2

THE TENT

As we grew older, Andre and I discarded The Lone Ranger and Tonto for Tonka Trucks. In Andre's backyard was a square patch of dirt perfect for playing Tonka trucks. Some of these Tonka trucks could move dirt, some could carry and dump piles of dirt, and some could even scoop up the dirt, swivel, and drop the dirt in a dump truck. We would make roads in the soil and design little construction sites. Moving earth and changing the layout of our tracks kept us busy for hours.

At home, I didn't have all the great toys that Andre had. My older brother, Cyril, was older than me by six years. He had a cool collection of Hot Wheels cars which he didn't really play with anymore. He let me know that while I could play with them, they were still his. The cars came in a green suitcase-styled box with a lid that snapped shut and read, "Hot Wheels" on the front of it. Inside the box, there were four rows of cars vertically and five rows of cars horizontally, and every available spot held a different type of car. It wasn't long before I had a favorite car out of the collection. It was a red 1980 Corvette Stingray. This car could fly, jump, and move at "warp speed" — a speed I heard about in the movie Star Wars my dad watched on the VCR.

I made my own fun. Along with playing with my brother's cars, I drew and coloured — and made forts. To build a fort in the downstairs TV room, I took the two cushions from the sofa and stood them up on their sides. Then I took the two cushions from the loveseat and placed them on top of the sofa cushions and rested them on the back of the sofa. Two small blankets draped over the sides of the couch completely enclosed my fort. If I needed to get out, I would simply lift the blanket and fold it over, and there was my opening, leaving the rest of the fort intact. I remember thinking I was pretty smart. It wasn't long after I learned that I could build such a fortress, that the thought of expanding my empire came to mind.

I connected another couch to my design and my empire grew to include half of the TV room. Then another idea came to mind—expanding my fort to include the whole TV! But that brought another question: how would I keep the center up?

I went upstairs and asking my mom for more blankets.

She asked suspiciously, "What do you need blankets for?"

"Oh, just building a fort, Mom," I replied.

"A fort?"

"Yes, Mom, a fort. Do you know where the broom is, Mom?"

"In the broom closet beside the fridge," she said.

I used the broomstick to keep up the center of the fort, like the centre pole in a circus tent.

Finally, I was done! I had a place for my favorite toys, a place to sleep, and little hiding places for my snacks.

Then, the unexpected happened. I heard my dad come home from work. I listened to the thud, thud, thud of his heavy work boots. I imagined him taking them off and placing them one by one on the back porch. I heard the creak of his chair as he sat down at the head of the table, which is where he always sat when he ate. My mom typically had a plate of food waiting for him, as he often worked overtime, coming home after the rest of the family had already eaten supper. On the night I first completed my fort, I heard his fork scrape the plate—this meant he was almost done with his meal. I heard him get up from the table, his footsteps coming towards the stairs that led to the basement. It wasn't long before he was down enough stairs to see that the whole basement was one big fort.

"Niall," he said in his deep stern voice.

"Yes," I replied.

"Take it down. I wanna watch TV."

"Aw, Dad ... I just finished building it."

"Take it down. Come on, I want to relax a bit and watch TV."

I didn't realize it at the time, but my dad had just finished a twelve-hour shift, and he wanted to relax after a long day of work. I didn't dare make my dad repeat himself a third time. I started to take down the fort. I put away all the blankets, pillows, and the books I used to weigh the tent down and keep the blankets from slipping off. Naturally, I was upset.

"Dad, I really wanted to sleep in my fort tonight!"

I stomped upstairs to my room and played with Cyril's cars.

I built and tore down that fort over and over. I mastered how to make it and tear it down before my dad got home and wanted to watch his TV shows. It was like clockwork—no fuss and no disappointment. I soon learned that if I enjoyed building it, I could get the same joy from having it cleaned up for my dad when he came home from work and wanted to watch his shows or movies.

Sometimes, when he was done watching his films and had retired upstairs, I came downstairs and set up the fort again; eventually, I knew I would be able to sleep in it, which was my ultimate goal.

One evening, I thought I had reached that goal, but the thrill was short-lived.

I had settled into the fort when my mom came down and said, "Niall, what are you doing down there?"

"I am playing in my fort," I replied.

"It's eight o'clock, come up and have a bath, and then it's time for bed."

When my mother wanted me to do something, there was precious little room for negotiation. Although she always spoke lightly and her voice had a sweet ring to it, she had a way of saying things in a manner that you couldn't argue with, even if you wanted to. I would say, "Okay, Mom." There may have been a few rare occasions when I said, "Okay, Mom, just five more minutes." But the request, if granted, was soon followed by her voice, calling down to me in the basement, "Okay, Niall, you asked for five minutes, and it has now been ten."

After bath time, my mom always had my pajamas ready. They would be nicely folded, placed on the fourth or fifth step going upstairs, along with a clean pair of "undies." I loved bath time; I would take my toys and put them in the bathtub with me and play until the water turned cold. Another thing which brought me great joy was taking some of the bubbles from the bubble bath and putting them on my face as if I had a beard and a mustache. I am unsure if my dad wore a beard back then or where I got the idea from, but I can remember scooping the bubbles in my little hands and putting the bubbles on my face. This always brought a smile from ear to ear!

After bath time, my mom would allow us a bedtime snack. Apple slices, peanut butter and banana sandwiches, peanut butter and jelly on toast, or the occasional bowl of cereal. After the snack, upstairs to bed I went.

I shared a room with my brother, Cyril. I would open the door to see him reading his *Archie* comics. Behind him was a collection of novels, including *The Hardy Boys*, which was a group of boys that solved mysteries. Stickers of his favorite bands, in two-inch squares, decorated the backboard of his bed: Iron Maiden, Metallica, U2, Sex Pistols, Led Zeppelin, ZZ Top. He found the sticker prizes in bags of Old Dutch potato chips.

I was more into superheroes at the time. I had a superhero bed sheet—Batman, Superman, Wonder Woman, and The Flash!—that was handed down to me from my brother. He even gave me a few superhero comics which he didn't read anymore. He had become more interested in *Archie* comics and the Hardy novels.

I would fly Superman around and make whooshing sounds. I would race Superman and the Flash; both were as fast as a speeding bullet, so it was often a tie. Sometimes, I made Superman win in slow motion. I would create amazing fight scenes with the two superheroes colliding. Depending on the day, I varied who won. Sometimes Superman would win and other days it would be the Flash. Batman had some pretty good run-ins with Superman every so often too.

When it was time to turn off the light and go to bed, my brother always made sure that I was tucked in and comfortable.

He would say, "Are you good?"

"Yep," I would reply.

"Okay, close your eyes."

I would close my eyes, and I would hear Cyril take a couple of steps and jump into his bed. It wasn't long after that I would hear the click of his bedside lamp come on. I would sit up and look across the room.

"Niall go back to sleep," he would say. Of course, I would— or at least try to anyway. I always looked up to my older brother. As I pretended to sleep, I could hear the pages of the book turning as he read.

3

THE DREAM

When I fell into dreamland, I would often have the same dream. It was in the home I lived in as a child, a 900-square-foot, war-time house with three bedrooms upstairs. The main level had a living room, dining room, laundry room, and kitchen.

My dream was based on the popular story, *The Three Little Pigs*. It started with footsteps outside of the house, which would wake me within my dream. When my eyes opened, I was frozen with fear. I settled my breathing, slowing it down so I could listen clearly.

I heard the *stomp, stomp, stomp* of the big bad wolf walking towards the house. Everyone inside the house scattered and went to find a place to hide. By everyone, I mean the three little pigs and myself. One pig hid behind the long green curtains in the living room which hung from the ceiling to the floor. Another pig hid in the laundry room, underneath a pile of laundry. As for the third pig, he hid under one of the living room couches. I could clearly see him from my position huddled under a chair in the dining room.

Stomp, stomp, stomp. We all heard the big bad wolf approach the house. I heard him rattle the doorknob. There was a long creaking sound as the door swung open. *Stomp, Stomp.* He entered the living room. There was a five-second pause with no movement in the entire house. The only sound I heard was from the wolf: heavy breathing followed by a low, deep growl.

Thud, thud, thud. A long pause followed by a growl. The sound of him licking his chops, slurping up saliva as it dripped off his large, sharp teeth. A short growl. He started walking down the hallway. The floor creaked with each step. He headed toward the kitchen, and then paused. A new growl came. This growl was different, as if something had caught his attention.

I focused on not moving a muscle and not making a sound. I lay ever so still.

Stomp, stomp, stomp.

I heard him walk through the kitchen. He was walking in my direction. He stopped at the doorway leading into the dining room. I couldn't see him, but I most definitely heard his slow, low growl.

My eyes were glued to the doorway. I waited for him to step further and enter the dining room. I remember thinking: *This is it. I will be caught. Slaughtered. Chewed up. Ripped apart.*

Stomp, stomp.

He stepped into the dining room but continued through to the living room. He had a long bushy tail, almost-black fur with areas of dark and light grey. He was very tall and thin. He looked hungry.

Once in the living room, he stopped. I saw his head turn left and scan back to the right, searching for his next meal. His attention focused on movement from the curtain; something had caught his eye. He let out a deep growl, louder than all the rest, and headed towards the curtain.

I had to close my eyes. I couldn't bear to see what was about to happen. I only heard the high-pitched squealing and yelps, and the sound of tearing flesh from bones.

Then the high pitch squeals stopped. My eyes were still shut tight. I heard a thud on the floor as if something dropped from the wolf's grasp. I imagined that it was the carcass of the mauled pig's lifeless body.

Stomp. Stomp.

The wolf stepped toward the laundry room. "I can smell

you; I know there are more of you," the wolf said in a chilling, deep, snarly voice.

He stopped in the doorway which led into the laundry room. The wolf was out of my sight, but I could hear him sniffing loudly. Then came the growl again.

The sounds of the vicious attack within the laundry room were over quickly; short yelps, a squeal, and then silence. There was no sound of anything hitting the floor. Maybe the pig was dropped on a pile of clothes, cushioning its fall.

Then there was only one pig left, and he was in the same part of the house as I was.

I should try to move to another spot, I thought. But I was scared stiff, unable to move.

Stomp, stomp, stomp, stomp.

I heard the quick, heavy steps as the wolf left the laundry room and went into the kitchen.

Stomp, stomp, stomp.

Before I knew it, he was standing in the middle of the dining room. The wolf headed in my direction and then stopped in front of my hiding spot. I held my breath, holding myself as still as possible. The wolf leaned down, and I could see the tip of his nose and part of his mouth come into view.

"Sniff, sniff, sniff," followed by the low terrifying growl. "Sniff, sniff, sniff."

I heard fast running.

Stomp, stomp, stomp, stomp.

His paws pounded against the floor and across the room. He threw the couch into the air and began mauling the third little pig, snarling while he ripped the limbs off the smaller animal. I could hear teeth ripping through the pig's body. It was so loud. He was only ten feet from where I still hid.

Loud screams came from the little pig. Horrifying screams.

Then everything stopped. There was a long pause. Finally, the wolf began to turn slowly toward me; he had blood around his mouth and dripping from his chin. He let out a long, slow growl.

As he completed the turn, his foot pivoted to the right and started to walk toward me. He approached my hiding spot and then continued past me, exiting the house through the back door. He left it wide open. Once he was outside the house, I remained still. Once I was sure he was gone, I slowly came out from underneath the chair.

That is when I would always awake from the dream.

That dream haunted me into adulthood. In some ways, it mirrored my life. Each time, just before absolute death or destruction, I narrowly escaped. But eventually, escape was not going to be an option. Eventually the *stomp stomp stomp* would be for me.

4

SCHOOL

I had a relatively normal childhood growing up; I did all the things an average boy would do. I rode my bike, played at parks—and being Canadian, I played a lot of hockey. Until the beginning of Grade 3, I attended a local school at the far end of the next block from where I lived. It was a large school made entirely of bricks on the outside, and it reminded me of a castle. In the schoolyard, there was a full-sized hockey rink where my dad would often coach my brother, Cyril, in the evenings and on weekends. Across from the rink, there was a play area with a fort made from wooden telephone poles. This is where we all played as kids. We would run across the bridge, up the stairs, and down the fireman's pole on the side of the fort. There was a concrete pad with painted lines that we used for the game Four-Square and hopscotch.

I have always been outgoing and could connect with different personalities—both boys and girls. The first girl that I can remember spending any time with was Robyn, who I met in the school yard playing hopscotch. We often played at her house. Our house was across the alley and five houses down from Robyn's place, so it was easy for my mom to call me home.

Mom would yell from the backyard of my house, "Niall … supper time!"

I would yell back, "Okay, coming!"

I would run home and eat as fast as I could because I wanted to get back to Robyn's to play. When it started to get dark, we could always expect another yell from my mom.

Sometimes she would call Robyn's mom, Marleen, who would then come to the stairs and yell, "Niall, that was your mom, and she wants you to go home." Robyn would come outside and walk me as far as she was allowed.

In 1986, at the end of Grade 2, our neighbourhood school closed and Robyn and I went to different schools at the beginning of Grade 3—a change that didn't affect our after school routine. After classes, I was excited to come home and call her as soon as I could—from the old rotary phone attached to the kitchen wall. The conversation was never very long. We were very direct as kids.

A conversation might have sounded like this:

"Hello, is Robyn there?"

Her older sister Monique, who would often answer the phone, would yell, ""ROBYN!"

Before too long, I would hear Robyn's voice on the phone, "Hello."

"Hey, Robyn, what are you doing?" I would ask.

"Oh hey, I was just coloring, wanna come over and colour?"

My reply was always a fast and blunt, "Okay, bye," and off I went.

I would take off fast, not even asking permission from my mom. But she knew exactly where I went. Mom would often call for me to come home for supper or that it was getting late, but sometimes she would come walking down the alley in her bare feet on the gravel lane to fetch me. (Robyn and I still don't know how my mom did that! I couldn't take two steps on the gravel without wincing in pain. My mom is a tough woman.)

⸺

Another girl that was special to me from a young age was Pamela, who I met when I transferred schools at the beginning of Grade 3. I liked Pam from the moment I saw her. I don't know if it was because she was the same colour as I was, or because of her perfect skin, or her long beautiful hair. My eyes always seemed to follow her wherever she went. I am not sure why, but I was intimidated by her. I would choose a desk facing her, but that wasn't too obvious. That way, I could look at her without her noticing. I had a real crush on her, and everyone knew it . Unfortunately, my affection wasn't reciprocated—I guess I just wasn't her type. Pam hung around a core group of friends. These were the "cool girls" of the class and were inseparable. I was friends with all of them, which allowed me to hang with Pam.

Pam joined my church group, which allowed me to get to know her in a different setting, free of her group of popular girls. What do you think I did with this great opportunity? I decided to be a prankster and do something silly to Pam. When she was in my house for a church function, I decided to play the gentleman and got Pam a chair. Pam responded, saying, "Oh, thanks." When she started to sit, I pulled the chair out from underneath her. It set her off balance, and she tumbled to the floor. I only did it for a laugh, but I later learned it was quite embarrassing for her. I initially thought I shouldn't do it, but then I did it anyway. When I saw her hit the floor, I realized what I did, and I felt horrible.

This wasn't the first time my impulsive nature had backfired. In Grade 2, I was playing on the fort next to the rink during recess. We would jump from a specific area of the fort and land in the soft sand, using a tuck and roll technique. When it came my turn to jump, I was more impatient than usual. There was a girl in front of me who was sitting on the edge of the fort. She was unsure if she wanted to jump. I decided to assist her in making her long, drawn out decision. I pushed her. She didn't land quite right and started crying. I was called into the principal's office for a stern lecture. I felt horrible for what I had done. I didn't apologize that day, but when she returned to school a few days later, she was wearing a cast on her right arm. I walked up to her and told her that I was very sorry and asked if we could still be friends. She smiled and accepted my apology.

Transferring to a new school in Grade 3 opened up a whole new world of friendships. After my first day of school, I walked with my new friend, Dan, to his house to play. We became the best of friends even though he was in my sister Nola's grade which was one year ahead. Along with Dan, I met other great friends which I am still in contact with today like Paul, Matthew, Tyler, James, Justin, Alex, Mia, Pam, and Chelsea. These were my core group of friends and we all participated in all the usual things children do at schools, spending our recesses running around and playing in the school grounds. It is safe to say that growing up was a lot of fun.

I had been born with a permanent, lifetime disability called Fetal Alcohol Spectrum Disorder (FASD), a condition that affects a person's brain. My parents were told that my birth mother drank during her pregnancy with me and that had been the cause of my disability. In Grade 4, my symptoms of FASD, particularly my behavioral issues and speech challenges, became more obvious.

I was unable to pronounce my "R's" correctly; if I was going to say the word "red," I would instead say "wed." I was put into a special class, away from all the other students for a few hours of the school day. My teacher would put a popsicle stick on my tongue and push it back slightly, allowing the right sound to come out of my mouth. It took a while, but I was eventually able to correct my speech.

Besides my impulsiveness, other behavioral issues and learning disabilities would soon manifest themselves and these would persist into my later school years and beyond. Although I have developed strategies to work around my disability, FASD is a lifetime diagnosis.

In 1991, in Grade 7, I had a particular teacher who I was constantly in trouble with and as a result was often sent to the principal's office. One time, the teacher had given me recess detention, but it slipped my mind. When the recess bell rang, I ran outside with my friends. During a game of tetherball, the teacher yelled at me to return inside for detention. Frustrated with me, he threw me down on a bench. His force resulted in my head being smashed against the brick wall behind me. My bell was rung and I felt fuzzy. I didn't cry but I do remember him yelling ferociously at me, telling me how frustrated he was with my actions. I was put into a side room, that resembled a broom closet, for the remainder of the day.

⸻

In 1992, towards the end of grade 8, our thoughts turned to preparing for our graduation ceremony. To my surprise, I was told that I was to be awarded the sportsmanship award at the graduation ceremony. However, I almost didn't receive it—thanks to my impulsive behavior. We were in a classroom, waiting to be told to head down to the gym for the ceremony. We were goofing around, excited to be graduating from Grade 8 to high school. I picked up a foam brush, one of the ones used to wipe the chalkboard. I thought the foam brush was foam through and through; I was mistaken. I threw it, in hopes of tagging another classmate, but it hit my friend Adam in the back of the head. I soon found out that there was a piece of wood in the middle of the foam brush, and when it struck Adam, it busted on the back of his head. Although Adam wasn't really hurt, my teacher took me outside and cursed at me. Yelling, she let me know that I should have my award taken away from me, as my actions showed that I didn't deserve such a reward.

My FASD had begun to truly shape how I interacted with others.

5

HOCKEY AND BMX DREAMS

I played hockey from the age of six until I was about fifteen. I was a small and skinny kid and always the smallest on my team. Many of my best friends played Tier 1, but I didn't make it through the Tier 1 tryouts. I usually played Tier 2 or Tier 3 hockey. I wasn't the greatest, but I did pretty well, averaging 35 to 50 goals per year.

One of my favourite hockey memories is of my first tournament. I remembered the mornings my dad opened the bedroom door to wake my older brother for his hockey tournaments. Now it was finally my turn! I was so excited. On the night before the tournament, my dad tucked me into bed, saying "Okay Niall, close your eyes and get some rest. You have a big day tomorrow, and we have to be up early for the tournament." In the morning, he came to my bedroom door and quietly whispered, "Niall, get up. We need to get going soon."

I headed downstairs and found my dad putting the finishing touches on a breakfast that he had prepared for me. (When Dad made breakfast before hockey, it was always toast with cheese whiz and strawberry jam, and a glass of milk or a glass of tomato juice. I never really enjoyed eating what my dad prepared but I ate it anyway. I eventually told him that I really preferred peanut butter and jam sandwiches, but he didn't change the ingredients. I always got the same thing. I just accepted it because I knew my dad was making sure that I ate something before playing hockey.)

When we arrived at the rink for our hockey games, we would head straight to the locker room. All the dads were there to dress their kids for the game. My father was a strong man and I never stepped onto the ice with loose skates. He always made sure that my equipment was secure and that I was comfortable. He would strap my mask on my helmet and tell me to skate hard and to have a good game and to dig for the puck.

I wasn't the best player on the team, but I was always up there in the top couple of players. I often received "Player of the Game" for our team, which made me proud. I felt I owed it to my dad and to my team to always try my best. Sometimes after a whistle of a play, I was called to the boards. My dad would walk to the end of the tall glass so that he could give me advice. He would tell me to keep my head up, to keep my stick on the ice, and to head to the front of the net to look for a pass. When I listened to his coaching advice, I was successful in scoring goals and assisting other teammates in their scoring.

One year, my dad was frustrated with the coach, who was the father of my friend Everett. The coach benched me for scoring a goal. I was on a breakaway and skating down the left side of the ice. Everett was across the ice on my right side. I knew Everett was there, but I took a wrist shot, aiming for the corner of the net. The puck sailed top shelf, right over the goaltender's glove and I scored. When I returned to the bench, the coach benched me for not passing the puck to Everett. After the game, I was stripped of the captain's "C" from my jersey. All because I didn't pass the puck to the coach's son. I was given the "A" and made Assistant Captain of the team. This demotion hurt. As far as I knew, my job as the captain of the team was to lead us to victories. I was a team player with assists and goals. When it came to passing the puck, I knew I was doing my part.

The following year, my dad and his friend coached our team. I scored my most memorable goal that year. I believe it was the fastest and greatest goal I have ever scored. When the puck dropped, I poked it through the legs of the opposing player and hopped around him quickly as the defense started to work themselves towards me. My speed drove me as I split through both defensemen. Before I knew it, I was on a breakaway and shot the puck over the goalie's glove. The play could not have been more than five seconds from when the puck dropped till I put it in the net. It was one of my most memorable hockey moments and the one of which I'm the most proud.

———

In Grade 7 and 8, I often went to the BMX track on the corner of Ruth and Lorne Avenue, which was only a few blocks from my house. The BMX track attracted a lot of neighbourhood kids. It was a community support type of sport. The kids would meet up and cheer on the BMX riders. I wasn't racing at the time, but I wanted to. My brother raced; he had a yellow number "1" plate on his bike. He would sometimes come home with trophies and plaques. Some were first-place finishes and others second or third place. He was a fairly good racer, and people would cheer him on from the stands.

There was one family of racers that dominated the BMX scene in Saskatoon. They were the Cane family: Jeremy, Ivan, Jim, Mark—and Soloman, the youngest of the brothers and closest to my age. Jim Cane was a fast rider. No one could beat him. He occasionally had wipeouts, but for the most part, he was the king of the track. Jim's younger brother, Mark, was also a powerhouse and very fast!

I really liked to watch the Soloman brothers on their bikes. They inspired me to try harder as a rider. Sometimes I went to the track to watch them practicing—as the performed gate starts and mastered their jumps. I watched how they peddled into the berms and how they stopped briefly to take the corners and then hammered on the peddling as soon as they were almost out of the corners. I complimented them on their high level of skill and asked a lot of questions.

I remember the day that Mrs. Cane was selling one of their old BMX bikes, a Mini Norco Spitfire, for $175. I didn't have any money to buy this bike, so I took jobs around the house to earn cash. It took longer than I wanted to save up the money I needed. I knew

Mrs. Cane was going to sell the bike by a specific day, but as the day approached I still didn't have enough money.

When I came home from school that day, I told my mom that if I didn't buy the bike that day, it would be sold to another rider from the track. My mom explained to me that I hadn't earned enough money for the bike and so I wouldn't be able to purchase it. I wanted that bike so badly. I begged her for the money, but Mom said she didn't have it. In my head, that seemed impossible. How could she not have—what seemed to me—such a small amount of money? I was very upset by her decision.

I walked to Soloman's house to let Mrs. Cane know that I really wanted the bike and I was close to having the $175. I told her that I was working hard to earn the amount needed, but I only had $150. I think it was obvious to Mrs. Cane how badly I wanted the bike, so she sold it to me for the $150 I had.

I was so happy! I rushed home to show my mom the bike that I had worked so hard for. It came with all the pads that I needed so I could race. The only thing I needed was a number plate. As I had no more money, I used a styrofoam dinner plate that I got from the track, wrote my number on with a black Jiffy marker, and attached it to the bike with plastic zip ties.

When I first started at the BMX track, I encountered challenges. I was a bit scared of the starting gate. The gate was on top of a hill and it had a steep decline that gave racers initial momentum, allowing them to reach a high speed quickly. Immediately after reaching this speed, the racers met a bump in the track. If that bump wasn't taken properly, a racer could be airborne. For the most part, this stage was where riders wiped out.

After school and most evenings, I practiced, eventually developing the skills necessary to place in the top three, just as my brother had before me.

When I outgrew my BMX, I bought a Diamondback. By this time I had a paper route which met my financial needs for my growing BMX career. My Diamondback was a heavier, chrome-moly frame bike. Sometimes, I rode my bike to the track, but then just sat on the bleachers and watched what more experienced riders were doing. I make mental notes about what I would try after the track cleared out. There was something about practicing on the track over and over that brought me great satisfaction; I knew that every time I went around it, I got better.

Over the years, I owned a couple of other bikes. One was an Elf Limo Double Cross which I bought from the Cane family when I was fifteen. It was around this time that I inherited the name "Scooby-Doo Schofield." The World BMX Racing Championships was held on the last couple days of the 1997 Saskatoon Exhibition. At the Ex, I won a big Scooby Doo stuffed animal and was carrying it to the track when my friend Maverick yelled, "Here comes Scooby Doo-bilicious." That friend still calls me "Scooby-Doo Schofield" when he encounters me at the local BMX track.

With practice, I accumulated enough points at the local Saskatoon track to qualify to race at the national level. I was excited! Although I was racing against elite riders, I was there to try my best, and that was all that mattered to me. I didn't place, but I really enjoyed the experience. After I was eliminated, I retreated to the bleachers and became a spectator, cheering on riders from my home track. It was a fun and exciting weekend. It was the only national event I ever participated in and afterwards I decided to stay in the sport only at a local level.

Shortly after the national event, I was involved in a car accident, taking me out of BMX. Now with severe back problems, I was no longer able to ride. I sold my bike to another rider who I knew would appreciate its quality and get good use from it. I was frustrated that I couldn't ride anymore, but I still went to the track to support other riders and watch their progress.

After months of rehabilitation and physiotherapy, I was able to walk without pain. Eventually, thanks to rehab and pain medications, I was able to again ride a bike.

At this point, I didn't have a bike so I asked Damian if I could ride his from time to time. He was okay with me borrowing the bike, but he always reminded me to be careful and not to injure myself. Over time, he lost interest in BMX, and I bought his bike.

Now able to ride, I decided to start racing again. I was excited to sign up at the clubhouse, but at the back of my mind, I was cautious. As I wrote my name on the entry form, I wondered what would happen if I re-injured my back. I practiced a few gates, and my back felt well enough, although I didn't crank the pedals hard. I knew that I wasn't 100% and that I couldn't push myself. I was just happy to ride on the track again. I went around the track repeatedly to warm up.

I felt good enough to race, so I did. I kept up with the other racers, but never pushed to gain spots. Maverick announced the races, and I still chuckle at the thought of his voice over the mic, calling the race as he saw it and saying, "...and here comes Scooby-doo coming around the berm from the inside and down the stretch, Scooby-doo takes the number two spot." It didn't matter to me where I placed. The only thing that mattered was that I was riding again.

The next day, I awoke in pain. I quickly reached for my pain medication. I had medications for pain and more pills for inflammation.

I kept racing, but it didn't take too many events for me to realize that my racing days had come to an end. My injuries were too severe.

6

JOHN

As early as Grade 3, I started to exhibit behavior problems. Part of these problems were no doubt due to the FASD, but there was something else also at work. Something horrible. Something big. Something that would affect my life's trajectory.

Despite the many wonderful memories of my childhood, they are clouded by the loss of something valuable to me. My innocence. My young childhood was shattered and my life became engulfed in dark thoughts as a result of this loss.

When I was eight, my cousin John would often come to the city and visit Cyril. He was my brother's best friend. One evening my parents were out—at a Bible study or for coffee with friends. On this particular night, I remember having a bath, as I would usually do before bed. When I came upstairs from my bath, my brother and my cousin were in my parents' room, sitting in front of a mirror. My brother Cyril had a comb in his hand. He was carefully parting his hair precisely down the center. What my brother would do, of course, John would do as well.

When it was time for me to go to bed, it was John who tucked me into bed. I do not know where my brother was; all I remember is that my cousin and I were alone. He put me under the covers and then got in bed beside me. He removed his pants and pushed my head towards his crotch. I didn't know what was going on, but I can remember him telling me to put my mouth on his penis, telling me that it was okay. I can still remember the feeling of his hand, guiding my head, and explaining how I was supposed to do whatever it was that I was doing. He moved my head up and down and coached me to watch my teeth.

This didn't happen just that once. It usually happened after my bath time and always when my other family members were occupied or absent. He picked his times carefully.

The place never changed, though. I shared a room with my brother; my bed was on the right side of the room, and my brother's bed was on the left. It always happened in my bed, and always with me under the covers and him on top.

For a few days after each abuse incident took place, thoughts rolled around in my mind as my young brain tried to dissect what exactly had happened. The only conclusion that I came to was that what took place was wrong.

In later years, counsellors I worked with told me that when something traumatic happens, the brain can often block it from your memory, and that is exactly what my brain did. However, in my teenage years, memories of what had happened would often come flooding back. My brain was no longer blocking the memories.

I had to talk to someone.

Knowing my mother's love for me, I decided to tell her what had happened. I eventually worked up the courage. As I spoke with her, I had feelings of shame soaring through me as I started to explain the actions that had taken place in my room with my cousin. After I was done speaking, I looked up. Her sadness was evident. I could see the disappointment in her face and watched her shoulders drop and then shrug.

Then she started to speak. She expressed that I should say nothing more of what had taken place in my room. If the rest of the family heard of this news, a great shame would affect all of the family. I can remember her index finger as she placed it on her lips and made the "shhhhh" sound. "Remember Niall" she said,

"You must never speak of this again. It will do more harm to the family than good."

I was advised to bury it deep within me. The importance of the family reputation was more important than my own mental health and well-being.

These abuse incidents created deep confusion in me. I was uncertain as to what a normal relationship between boys and girls, men and women looked like. I began searching out more female friendships with a subconscious curiosity for sexuality.

When I was ten, I shared my first kiss, with Robyn. We were best friends through and through. I can remember having romantic feelings for her. I wasn't aware, at the time, of how to act or how to feel about it, so I thought I would write her a letter. I tried to explain to her that she meant a lot to me and that I really liked her.

When I wrote the letter, I was confident that Robyn would simply say, "I like you too, Niall," and everything would be peachy. That wasn't the case at all. I remember standing in the driveway at her house, asking her to tell me how she felt about me. Did she feel the same as I did? I was young, but I knew that Robyn made me happy. I also knew that writing that letter scared me to death, but I wanted her to know how I felt. She told me that we couldn't be anything more than friends.

The next girl I had an emotional connection with was Hailey. I met Hailey when I was ten years old. She attended a church that was right across the street from my school. We talked on the phone quite often, and eventually, we grew to have feelings for one another. She is the first girl I kissed in a serious way.

We would meet halfway between her house and mine and go for walks and just really enjoy each other's time. We would talk and talk; we always had something to talk about. Sometimes we would lay in the grass in front of the church and talk.

Quite often, we would just gaze into each other's eyes. I would get lost in her eyes. We would slowly lean together and kiss passionately. I really enjoyed kissing Hailey. She had full lips, flawless skin, a cute little nose, and rosy cheeks. She was taller than me, and I remember having to shimmy up when lying beside her to see eye to eye. While these were innocent kisses, I was able to grasp that there were emotions behind kissing a person when you showed them respect.

7

FIRST JOINT

High school introduced me to the world of drugs. It started in Grade Nine. I had already tried alcohol, but I was totally unaware of substances like marijuana, cocaine, ecstasy, acid and LSD. My friend Johnathan and his friend Craig would often come to class red-eyed and laughing hysterically. They seemed to always be having such a great time. One day, I asked them if I could join them on the morning break for their walk to go "spin one up."

I watched as they lit the joint and took pulls off of it. They took little pulls, and then one big long drag while holding it in and saying, "Ere" and they would start to laugh. They would pass it back and forth a couple of times. When the joint was small, and in danger of burning their fingers, they would butt it out. They would keep the roach for later, combining the leftover pot with the remains of others to make a second-generation joint.

After watching the joint go back and forth between Craig and Johnathan, I finally interrupted, saying, "Yeah, hand it over."

They handed me the joint, and I began to puff on it, mimicking their earlier actions.

Well, was I in for a surprise! I coughed so hard, my throat hurt and my eyes watered. I could taste the awful taste of resin on my lips. It was gross.

Then a feeling came over me. Lightheaded and buzzed, I suddenly had a laid back, chilled presence. It was a dopey, fun feeling. Soon after, there was that laugh that I had heard so often. We three laughed hysterically at things that I am sure would otherwise not be funny. Time had stopped, and I was in a haze of drug-induced feelings.

Craig started to laugh hard.

"What's so funny?" I asked.

While trying to hold in laughter, he replied, "You have class in five minutes. Oooo!"

For a moment, I felt afraid. I had been having so much fun that I forgot that in a few minutes, I would have to go back to class and somehow act normal.

Then Johnathan laughed and said, "Yeah, good luck, Niall!" He had a grin on his face and smirked at Craig.

There was no way I could go to class in the state I was in. My next class was English. My teacher was a stern, but fair teacher. But not fair enough to put up with my state of being.

I asked Craig and Johnathan what they were going to do.

"We are going to the mall, to the arcade, to play video games," Craig answered.

I had never missed a class, but if they were going to skip class, so was I. I remember thinking, *What harm would be skipping one class do?*

We went to the mall and played video games. Street Fighter was the popular game at the time. We played until other students started piling into the mall from my school and from another school down the block. Soon lunch hour was coming close to an end, and it was time to head back for fourth period. I felt straight enough to go back to school. My next class was art, and I loved art class.

Smoking that joint was a turning point in my life. It was one of many impactful moments that lead toward how my life would unfold.

8

THE GYM

I felt the need to compensate for my small build. Drugs offered me some of that compensation. But so too did my journey into weight lifting. When I first started training, I was 5'6" and I weighed about 110 pounds.

Cyril had a set of old weights that were filled with concrete and covered in plastic. He had 25 pound weights for his curl bar and dumbbells which were five and ten pounders. Being that I was a small and skinny runt, my brother looked huge to me. One memory that sticks with me is watching my brother put a huge log on his back and running up and down the stairs from the basement. It log looked heavy and the exercise intense. After that, he would do a wall press half squat where he would lean against the wall like he was sitting in a chair. It was a strenuous exercise. At that time, I was probably ten or eleven years old. I didn't know exactly what he was doing, but I knew that he lifted often and always worked out in a white undershirt.

My BMX bike buddy Soloman Cane lifted weights too. He had weights like Cyril's, but he also had a flat bench and a long bar for the bench press. Soloman invited me to start training with him. He was a year younger than me, but he was considerably bigger and it was quite obvious that he was benefitting from weight training. We would work out at noon at the school and if we didn't have the chance to work out at noon, we made sure we made it to the gym after classes.

One of Soloman's favourite exercises was the bench press. I couldn't lift anywhere near the weight that Soloman could. He was doing two 45-pounders per side, which is 225 pounds when using the Olympic-styled bar. The bar weighed 45 pounds by itself. I started with 25 pounds on each side, which was 95 pounds with the bar.

My art teacher was an ex-bodybuilder who had competed professionally. She had pictures from when she was in her prime and I was in awe of the impressive shape she was in. I was amazed that she developed such strong definition and physique just from lifting weights. I asked her questions about why she enjoyed lifting weights and what the benefits were. The world of fitness was opening and unfolding before my eyes.

I used the school gym for about eight months until I started attending the Saskatoon Field House. It had a full track, basketball courts, tennis courts, a rehabilitation center, and a weight room. By the time I moved to the field house gym, I had begun to grow, though not as quickly as I would have liked. I was the same height, but my weight was closer to 117 pounds. I would ride my bike home after class and change as fast as I could so I could get to the field house gym before it got too busy. I would have just enough time to get home after the workout to be on time for dinner. From time to time, I convinced other friends to join me, but none of them ever stuck it out or attended it as regularly and consistently as I did. My dedication and drive toward the gym grew stronger and stronger. Weight lifting was playing a significant role in my life.

9

THE ACCIDENT

My parents drove a little Ford Festiva. It was white in color, and my mother loved it, probably because it was a smaller car and good on gas.

My sister and I had gone on a ski trip with a group from our church. When my dad came to pick us up, I jumped into the front, and my sister sat in the back. My seatbelt was undone. I hadn't fastened it before we started moving. I was holding my coffee in one hand and my dad's coffee in the other. My dad asked us questions and my sister and I talked about some of the highlights from the trip.

As we got farther away from the church, we turned onto a busy street. I remember that we had just passed a hospital and we were coming up to a gas station on my right. While looking ahead, I could clearly see that the light was green. My dad was traveling the speed limit, which was fifty kilometers per hour. An older half-ton truck was approaching us from the other direction, signaling a left turn. It was wintertime, and the roads were extremely icy. I thought the truck would stop soon as we had the right of way, but for whatever reason, it didn't slow down, let alone stop. The truck turned left on a solid green light right in front of us. There was no way we could stop in time to avoid it.

My dad hit the brakes, and we started to slide. We slid directly into the center of the truck. Everything started going in slow motion, and I remember thinking: This is going to hurt real bad.

At the point of impact, my body flew forward and my head hit the windshield. When I recoiled back into my seat, I remember hearing my father cursing and my sister screaming about the pain in her chest. I could see that my dad's thumbs were bent awkwardly. Whether he was feeling the pain of his injuries was unclear, but his fury over the accident was crystal clear. After asking if we were okay, he exited the vehicle. I thought he was going to go talk to the other driver, and I was sure, at this point, that the driver of the other vehicle was in even more danger.

I will never understand why, but I got out of the vehicle and walked to the gas station that was across the street. I was in shock and really didn't know what was going on. I do know that I attempted to buy some five-cent candies with no money in my pockets to pay for them. When I went up to the cashier to try to pay, the clerk asked if I was okay.

"Yes," I replied, "Why do you ask?"

"You have blood running down your forehead," the clerk said.

The clerk gave me a piece of paper towel for my cut, handed me a few pieces of candy and then walked me back to the scene of the accident before returning to his store.

We sat there to wait for the police and the tow truck. When the tow truck came, our car was declared undrivable and we got a ride home with the tow truck driver.

I was 15 years old and this the first of many accidents that would affect my back and create long-term pain.

10

CYRIL

On June 8th, 1993, my life changed forever.

I was in Grade 10 and my brother was living in Vancouver. He had graduated from high school and had moved with the love of his life, Loretta, to the coast.

On Sunday, June 6th, Cyril had called home to catch up with the family. I was sitting on the couch in the living room, waiting patiently for my turn to talk to him. When we finally spoke, he suggested that he would buy me a ticket to fly out to Vancouver. I could come to see him for my birthday which was on August 23rd. I remember the conversation as clear as day.

He said, "Hey, Niall, how would you like to come out to Vancouver for your birthday?" "What, really?" I was excited.

"Yeah, you can come out, and I can show you what I like to do out here and throw a little party for you to meet some of my friends."

I was very excited!

"I will talk to mom and ask her if it is okay, and I will see you then, okay?"

"Okay," I said.

"Okay, I better get going. Put Mom back on. Behave yourself."

I went to bed that night thinking how lucky I was that I was going to get to see my big brother in Vancouver, a place that I had never been.

My house was about four kilometers straight west from my high school. My mom would often pack me a lunch, but I sometimes would forget my lunch and have to buy some fries from the school cafeteria, or go to the mall which was only a five-minute walk. I never went home for lunch. But for some reason on Tuesday, June 8th, 1993, when once more I forgot to bring my lunch to school, when the third period ended, I started jogging home for lunch. I knew the time would be tight, but I thought I would be able to get back in time for class.

When I walked into the house, I was confused and shocked to see so many family members there. Everyone should have either been at work or school. My aunt, sister Amber, mom, grandma, and others were there.

My sister Amber was crying. Amber crying was kind of normal, as she would often cry from cramps. But as I walked through the house, I noticed that everyone, not just my sister, was upset.

I asked, "What's going on?"

No one said a thing. I remember my auntie looking right at me, her lips clenched tight. I could instantly feel she felt sad, but she didn't say anything.

"What's going on?" I said again.

I don't know who said it, but I heard a voice say, "You have to tell him, Amber, you go."

I can remember my sister coming up to me. She pulled me into her room, which was on the main floor between the kitchen and the living room.

She closed the door and said, "Niall, sit down."

I sat down on the bed, and she said to me, "Niall..."

"What??"

"Niall...Cyril is dead. He was killed in a car accident last night."

I sat there, stunned. I don't think I even flinched. I thought: I just heard Cyril's voice a few days ago. He said he would see me soon. I was going to see him for my birthday.

I didn't hug my sister. I didn't cry. I got up from the bed, walked out of my sister's room, and I went downstairs to my room. When I got there, I sat on my bed. My brain was going a million miles an hour with many thoughts. Was this a dream? What did I hear? Could it be true, and if it was, how so? I had just talked to him. How could he be there one minute and gone the next? I remember thinking: No, this can't be true it just can't be.

I decided to go back to school as if nothing had happened. I thought: When I come back home, it will all be gone. All the people upstairs will be gone. Cyril won't be dead and everything will be normal.

And that is precisely what I did; I went back to school.

I don't understand what happened next, but I can remember walking down the main hallway at school. The hallway was empty, except for a group of people sitting together on the floor. I walked past them. I don't think I was crying, but I must have had a sad, wimpy look on my face because after I had passed the group, I heard a comment come from one of the guys, "Look at that pussy, ha ha ha." And they all laughed.

Something in me snapped. I turned instantly saying, "What the FUCK did you just say?"

I walked back toward the group, and I grabbed the first one that I saw laughing at me. I threw hi m against a locker. I swung and punched him repeatedly. I finally grabbed his head and raked it up and down the steel serrated part of the locker. I was pulled off the student by a teacher.

She grabbed my arm and took me to the principal's office. I sat in the office in the little waiting area, and I wondered what had just happened? I didn't understand my actions. I was confused. I normally would have never done such a thing. I remember being scared of what discipline would come from such actions. Would I be kicked out of school? What about all my friends? What they would think? If I had to switch schools, I wouldn't see them every day.

I remember the door opened, and the principal said, "Have a seat."

"So, what happened?" she asked.

I explained to her exactly what had happened over lunchtime and what the student had said to me. To my amazement, the look of anger that was on her face soon changed to one of sympathy and understanding. She said, "Niall you shouldn't be here. You should be with your family. You can't be in the right state to be here. Niall you have to leave the school, you cannot be here."

"Am I kicked out?" I asked.

"No, but I don't want to see you here for seven days, and when you come back, I want to see you okay?"

"Okay," I said.

I thanked her for her understanding, and I walked out of the office. I don't remember where I went after, but the worst was still to come. The harsh reality hadn't truly kicked in. My brother was dead.

11

FUNERAL

When I returned home, there were even more people in the house. There were friends of my mother who had brought gifts which filled the kitchen table. My mother was sitting in her chair in the corner of the living room. It is even hard to think of her look, now, as I write this. She had such pain; I didn't understand the severity of the pain, but I knew it crushed me inside when I looked into her eyes. I will never forget that look.

Cars continued to pull up over the next few days. Some had travelled great distances to pay their respects to my mom and other family members regarding the loss of my brother.

I don't remember the planning of the funeral, but I do remember getting ready for the funeral. I dressed in my suit and made sure I looked my best, as I was going to see my brother for the last time — on earth anyway. I saw my Uncle Norman pull up in a rental car. He lives in British Columbia and had flown in for the funeral. He was a strong individual and a successful businessman. He entered the house and chatted; he made his rounds, talked to everyone, and made sure we were ready. It was time for the viewing where we could spend a little time individually and say our goodbyes to my brother.

Cyril's death was soon to become a reality. Up to this point, I still didn't think it was true. It was time. My Uncle Norman came to me, grabbed my shoulder, and suggested I ride with him. I felt privileged that he had asked me to accompany him while driving to the funeral hall. We exited the house and proceeded to walk to his car. It was black and shiny with beautiful leather seats.

"Buckle up," he said as he started the car.

We drove toward the freeway that crossed the river. I don't know if my Uncle Norman did this to lighten the mood, or if he even intended to do this, but when we entered the on-ramp to the freeway, he punched the gas. This sudden speed sent me firmly to the back of the seat; we were flying! I remember smiling along with my uncle; somehow, amid all the pain, it was my uncle who was able to bring a smile to my face.

The seriousness of seeing my brother in a casket suddenly hit me. I had never been in one of these places before, so I didn't know what to expect. We all sat in a little room outside of the room where Cyril lay. I remember it being hushed. I could hear whimpers of pain and see people wiping away their tears. My emotions were not like the others; why was I not crying? My turn finally came, and I was escorted into a room where my grandmother and mother were sitting.

As I walked into the viewing room, my brother's casket was on the left side of the room with the left side of it open so that you could see the top half of his body. In my hand was an envelope. I had written my brother a letter to take with him to the afterlife. These were the last words I would say to Cyril. I slowly walked up to the coffin. My eyes started at the foot of the casket and slowly moved up to his face, which was propped up by a pillow. His right hand was over his left. I placed the envelope on the side of the casket that was closest to me.

I leaned over to have a good look at my brother. The right side of his face didn't look much like the brother I remembered. There was a dent and ruffled rough skin near the temple area. The skin around his eye didn't look right. The left side of his face, on the other hand, was the face of the handsome brother I knew.

I reached out my hand and touched his chest. It was hard. I

touched his hair and around   his head. I felt the back of his head, but it was no longer there. When I felt that it was gone, my hand quickly moved away. I put my hand back on his chest, and it was at that point that I knew he was gone. When we left the funeral hall, we exited through the back where there were a couple of black limos waiting. After everyone had their chance to say goodbye, my brother was loaded into a hearse which we followed to the church. When we arrived at the church, it was packed full, and there were even people sitting in the balcony.

During the service, my father put his arm around me and leaned over. He said, "It's okay son ... it's okay, you can cry, it's okay," and rubbed my shoulder. I broke into tears. The tears slowly ran down my face as I looked at my brother's casket in the front of the church. I listened to the pastor bring the service to an end, and he called the pallbearers to the front, to carry Cyril out of the church. We proceeded to the Langham cemetery to lay him in the ground at his final resting place. I remember getting the opportunity to throw a few shovels full of dirt on top of the casket. I did not understand why, but I was glad I was given the shovel to do so.

12
AFTERMATH

After the death of my brother, many things happened that threatened to destroy the family. The grieving process was the hardest. It was crazy to watch my family fall apart. It was like a flower you see in perfect bloom, one that is full of life and colour. Its petals are full of water and soft to the touch, and then something happens, and the bloom quickly withers into a dry, lifeless flower, and the dead petals fall off until there is no life left.

When Cyril passed away, my mother laid in bed for weeks, which turned into months. She had always been a little overweight, but her weight drastically changed because she wasn't eating. If she wasn't upstairs in bed, she was in her favorite chair in the living room. She was grieving. I could not imagine a mother's pain of losing a son, her firstborn, her baby boy, the true bloodline to the family, the one to carry on the Schofield name. My brother's future had been so bright. A distance began, separating my mother and me. I watched from afar and saw her swallow herself up in sadness.

My dad and I drifted apart almost instantly. He took me out of hockey, and he put me into soccer. I was immensely upset by this. I asked him if I could please stay in hockey, even though I only lasted one indoor and one outdoor season. I later learned that my father found it extremely hard to keep me in hockey, as it made him think of the days when he took Cyril to hockey and coached him on the rink by the school. My father was a massive part of my brother's hockey activity as well as mine. I understood it was hard on my father to watch me play sports as it was an important part of his relationship with Cyril.

The distance grew between my father and I until we no longer spoke. It became uncomfortable. I started to feel like I could never be the son he wanted. I was not his bloodline; I was adopted. Feelings of doubt and low self-worth began to creep into my thoughts. School was no longer as important. I was pulled from the sport I enjoyed. My world, as I knew it, was crashing. Where there once was joy, there was only doubt and fear of not being wanted or loved. I had drifted out so far, soon I found myself all alone in the middle of nowhere.

Amber and I always had a respect for and understanding of each other. She always tried to help me. I believe it was because we were both close to Cyril that Amber was the one who broke the horrible news to me on the day he died. We would not drift apart.

After Cyril passed away, my relationship with my sister Nola crumbled. She was angry at the world. We couldn't communicate on a respectable level. There was a lot of fighting. We couldn't spend much time in each other's presence. But she was there for my mother and father through it all. It was always good between me and my little sister, Denise, I was now the only big brother she had and I tried to make sure she was okay.

As the early stages of grieving passed, new things began to fill my life. Where there was once joy, I found myself attracted to mischievousness and drugs. I rebelled against my Christian faith. I remember wondering: If there was a God, why would He let something like that ever happen to my brother? If God was the creator and gave life, why would He take my brother's life in such a way? It sounds so cliche now, but you don't see it when it is happening to you.

The loss of my brother was a huge turning point in my life. I had looked up to my older brother in every way. He was my hero. He taught me many things about hockey, BMX racing, baseball, football, skateboarding, weight lifting, and music. I was angered by the thought that God had taken my brother away. I couldn't understand why he was taken in such a violent way. I was taught that God has a plan for all of us. How could He plan such a horrible death for my brother?

During this time, I not only walked away from what I had been taught in church, I ran away. I ran to anything that could ease my pain. I was fifteen years old. I ran out of the arms of Jesus and straight into the arms of Satan like a bolt of lightning. I rebelled against all I believed to be true and right. I stopped attending church and spiraled downward. I did everything I was taught not to do — swearing, stealing, drugs, sex — and the worst of all, I did not, like the commandments stated, honor my mother and father. I ran far and for so long, I reached a point of complete emptiness and fear of the world. I lost who I was, and unconsciously damaged my true self in the process. There were no feelings of love, kindness, or self-worth. I was filled with anger, hate, emptiness, and pain. The devil had his claws deep into my soul, and he squeezed out every bit of light from my heart. This hell on earth consumed my life for many years. My life was changed and I searched for other alternatives to find my self-worth.

13

THE LAKE

After the loss of my brother, my cousin, John invited me to the lake as a means to lift my spirits and unwind. I was fifteen and excited to take some time away from the dreariness of my surroundings. I had buried any memories of sexual abuse from my younger years in the deep recesses of my brain. While we drove up to the lake in his black truck, he mentioned to me that my brother had lost his virginity up at the lake, and he suggested that it was time to lose mine.

John and I often played a game called "chip, crack, broken," which was a frisbee game. If you attempted to catch the frisbee and made contact, it was called a "chip," then if it happened again, a "crack," until you reached "broken" and the game would be over. One day at the lake, we returned to the cabin after a couple of games. John decided to nap, and I chose to go to the local concession, where two attractive girls were working. One girl, Samarah, was blonde and the other girl, Amy, was a taller and older brunette.

I took an instant liking to Samarah. She was nineteen and extremely attractive with an athletic build and long brown, almost black hair. Samarah and her friends were older than me. They drank beer and had late night fires at the beach.

On our second night at the lake, the group all went swimming at midnight. John had mentioned to me that they were going to be skinny dipping. Knowing this made me shy. I hadn't even hit puberty yet. I couldn't be seen naked in the presence of older guys. The early sexual abuse incidents were buried away, but subconsciously I had a heightened awareness regarding the dangers of being naked in front of males. There was no way I was going swimming naked. I went down to the beach hoping that Samarah would be there. Eventually, a tall female silhouette in the moonlight walked out of the water and was clearly walking in my direction.

I then heard a sweet voice say, "Niall?"

I replied, "Yep."

"Why aren't you swimming?" said Samarah.

"I'm not feeling it."

She came up and sat beside me. She was only wearing her bra and underwear. I could see goosebumps on her skin that formed in the cold midnight air. She suggested that I take my clothes off and come into the water with her. She said I could leave my underwear on. I was hesitant, but she stood up and reached her hand out to me. I held her hand, and she pulled me up from my seated position. As I removed my clothes, she headed toward the water, and as I watched her walk, I saw her black underwear had ridden up, leaving the bottom of her nicely shaped ass exposed. She stopped halfway to the water and turned back to make sure I was coming; I could see her large breasts perfectly. She stood at the edge of the lake where the sand turned into water, and she reached out her arm once again, waiting for my hand to grasp hers. We locked hands and walked into the water together.

Once we were deep enough, I completely immersed myself into the cold lake water. She did the same. When her head came out of the water, she had a big smile and her head was tilted back. She ran her hands over her hair, pushing it back and smoothing it out. We physically played in the water; throwing each other around and laughing. We were treading water while facing each other with smiles on our faces when she suggested we swim out to the dock that was further out on the lake. Once we reached the dock, we both held onto the edge with one hand while treading water with the other. We talked, looking up at moon and the stars that surrounded us. It was a beautiful clear night.

After a prolonged silent pause, Samarah said that I should come closer to her. She promised she wouldn't bite. She pulled me close to her and wrapped her long legs around my waist. This was all new to me, and I didn't have a clue how to react. I was nervous; so nervous that I was shaking. She noticed, and told me to relax. She leaned in and started to kiss me.

After our first kiss, she pulled back and said, "Not bad." She then guided me physically and gave me pointers on how she enjoyed being kissed. I got a play by play on different stages of kissing, which I needed because I was immature. Since she was older than me, it made sense that she had more experience and could lead. She told me that there are many types of kisses, and with each new one that she explained, she demonstrated how to do it.

There was the "peck" which was just a swift peck on the lips. The "smooch" was basically just like a peck but was held longer lip to lip. Then there was a "French kiss," which was an open-mouthed kiss where you put your tongue in her mouth. At first, I struggled with the French kiss business, but she explained in detail how much tongue you should use while kissing and how there should be chemistry in the act of kissing. When the French kiss felt right, and we were both equally engaged, a wonderful feeling came over my body.

She took my hand and placed it on her breast. Then the kissing stopped for a moment while she removed her bra and put my hand back on her bare chest. Her nipples were hard, and she pulled my lips down to her breast, placing my mouth over her nipple so I could lick and kiss its hardness. While I was enjoying her breasts, I felt her slowly rub her hand on my penis, over the top of my boxer shorts. I stopped what I was doing and pulled away. No woman had ever touched me there. She reassured me that everything was okay and politely asked me if I was alright. She spoke softly, telling me to relax.

I am not sure how I stacked up to other men in her past, but I definitely responded when she touched me. I felt surges of a pulsing feeling in my penis, and it seemed to get stronger the more she played with it until I was fully erect. She stroked my penis under the water while we kissed. Eventually, while I was again fondling her bare breasts, she guided my hand and placed it on her vagina. I was in complete shock. As my hand was upside down and rubbing the outer part of her vagina, she took my hand in hers and pressed my fingers inside of her. I remember her warmth and texture and how she felt different than the waters that surrounded us. We continued to kiss, and she eventually wrapped her legs around me again and with her free hand, grabbed my penis, and rubbed the tip of my penis on her vagina. She kept her hand on it, rubbing it back and forth on the outer part of herself until I had the tip of it into the opening of her vagina. She then drew herself to me, forcing my erect penis inside of her.

At this point, I had no idea what I was supposed to do. I didn't move, I was just inside of her. As we progressed, I slipped out a few times, and she put my penis back inside of her, but after a few more times of this, I lost my erection. I had just lost my virginity. It didn't last for a long time and I probably didn't do a great job but it was my first time and that was that.

Afterward, we talked for a bit longer while resting on the dock. People eventually yelled from the beach that they were going to leave, so we grabbed our underwear from the dock, and we headed in. Once we reached the beach, she gave me another kiss and disappeared into the darkness.

The next day I expected to see her at the concession, but she wasn't there. I was told that she would be back later that night. She was, and a group of us, including my cousin John, walked around the oval path, which was the main part of the park.

As Samarah and I walked together, a truck pulled up behind our group. The driver of the truck flashed its high beams and aggressively stopped close to the group before jumping out of the vehicle. He was a large man and wore a cowboy hat and blue jeans with a big belt buckle. He was angrily looking for someone. He started to run at me, and someone shouted, "Run!"

I was slow to recognize that it was me he was after, and by the time I started running, he was already at a full sprint. I dodged left and then right, trying to shake him, but I couldn't. I stopped hard and hit the ground, and he ran right past me. As soon as he had flown by me, I got up and quickly ran in the opposite direction. Once I had put a bit of distance between us, it wasn't hard for me to outrun him.

I was far enough away from him that John stepped between us and stood in front of him. He went toe to toe with the big country boy, who stood 6'3" and probably weighed 230 pounds. They exchanged hard punches. John came out on top, but he had some bruising on his face afterward. While we watched, friends of Samara told me that the angry guy was her boyfriend. I was very lucky that John was there because I was only 5'8" and 110 pounds and I wouldn't have come out of the fight with just a few bruises.

That weekend was the last time I went back to the lake. I was a different person in a couple of ways. Not only had I lost my virginity, after resuming my school activities, the strange feelings I had about being naked in front of guys continued. I never felt good changing in the locker rooms before and after gym class. I never showered with the rest of the guys; I would get changed and get out of there as fast as possible. One day, my gym teacher took it upon himself to make me shower. I was disturbed by this. He stood there after all the other students left, made sure I undressed, and sent me to the shower. I am not sure as to why he made it his duty to get me to shower with the other students, but I was angered and humiliated by this.

14

COCAINE

As I struggled with the loss of my brother and the change it made in my family life, I was searching to find myself. I began a lifestyle of heavy partying which ultimately resulted in significant drug use.

The first drug I tried, other than marijuana, was acid. LSD stands for lysergic acid diethylamide and it comes as a white powder or clear colorless liquid. It is a hallucinogenic that makes you high for roughly four to six hours, depending on the quality. LSD is a heavy drug, and it is challenging to be in a social environment if you have taken it. Your pupils dilate so much that it is difficult for someone to determine your eye colour

Although sometimes LSD made me intensely remember bad memories like Cyril's death, usually the acid allowed me to take my thoughts far away to a place where I didn't have to think about my family problems, the pain blanketed by a chemical imbalance induced by the drug. This was amazing for me.

Any time I felt the pain, I would call my friend Harrison. He was a burnout, a real groovy type of individual. Most people liked him because he was always laughing and for the most part was harmless. He was my initial LSD connection, Then I connected with others who were able to get different types of acid; white blotted, sugar cubes, and double hits.

Some people were crazy enough to put it right in their eyes. As for me, I stuck to putting it under my tongue; I was told that was the way it best absorbed into the body. I went to class a couple of times on acid. I think I was able to stay in class only once from the beginning to the end. For the most part, I would have to get out of there because it was just too intense. Things took on all sorts of shapes. My vision was messed up, and I couldn't focus. I would pick up my books and head out and just face the music from the teacher the next day. I had some crazy experiences while being on acid.

The first time I tried cocaine, I was at a party at Jason's, a popular guy from my high school. Things got crazy. Jason and I had split a twelve pack of a strong, 7% beer. I was sixteen years old, and I was super drunk. There were close to seventy-five people at the house, some older, some younger. Rob was Jason's younger brother and Mary was his older sister. A lot of my older friends were going in and out of a room upstairs so I decided to go up and check it out. I knocked on the door, but the room was quite full, and I had to wait to get in.

When I was finally allowed in, I saw a guy standing by a dresser. On top of the dresser, was a bunch of lines of a white powdered substance, which I would soon learn was cocaine. I remember being quite drunk, and I knew I had to go home in a couple of hours.

"Do you want a rip?" a guy asked.

My reply was, "Yeah, sure. I have never done it before, but yeah, I would be willing to try it for sure."

"Your pretty drunk bud, this will straighten you right out."

"Oh, really, how?" I asked.

"Just wait, you'll see," he replied.

Turns out, that was a valid statement.

We went over to the dresser. He took a card and pulled a line closer and handed me a Slurpee straw that was cut short. I put one end of the straw in my nose and the other to the pile of cocaine. While plugging one nostril, I inhaled fast and hard. It wasn't long after that I felt the effects of the drug take over my body. Everything became more precise. I was sharp and focused, and able to converse with others. I was no longer drunk or slurring. What an amazing feeling! I couldn't understand the pull at the time because it was a brand-new feeling to me. I just knew I liked it; it excited me so much that I wanted to seek it out again.

I called my mom and dad to come pick me up. Before they showed up, I must have chewed an entire pack of gum to hide the smell of alcohol and cigarettes. I tried to act as normal as possible. I am sure my parents could smell the scent of cigarettes on me as I entered the vehicle.

My mom asked her usual questions when I had been to a party, "Who was there? Was there a parent present or an adult?"

I politely replied, "Yep, there was." Mary was the oldest one there, so she was in charge. I think my parents were just happy that I called for a ride and that I was safe.

That was the start of my cocaine addiction. It started a lot like drinking did for me. When I started drinking, first it was only on the weekends. I was so excited for the weekends because I knew I would get smashed with my friends and do stupid things. Well, soon I had new goals to go along with the booze. I quickly learned that with a pinch of cocaine, my weekends would become so much better. I surrounded myself with people who could get it or the people who had it themselves and sold it to others. It was the ultimate drug; it grabbed hold and didn't let go. It was as if the devil himself grabbed my heart and soul and squeezed the life right out of me.

15

GYM TO CALL HOME

I was struggling in school. I wasn't focused on getting good grades, I was interested in meeting people and having fun and partying. I was dealing with the trauma of losing my brother by self-medicating and I was spinning out of control.

As I immersed myself deeper into the party scene, I continued my interest in weight lifting as I knew the benefits it had provided my brother during his life. In Grade 10, I had grown tired of the Saskatoon Field house and heard about a gym located on 8th St. in the Grosvenor Park Shopping Mall called Iron Works. I heard it had a strong focus on weight lifting, that it was hardcore with serious lifters who worked out there.

After entering the shopping center, I went down to the gym. All I could hear was the sound of steel clanking and weights dropping on the rubber mats. There was a smell; it was the smell of hard work, sweat, and — I am sure — some tears. I walked to the front desk, but no one was there. After a while, a large man walked up to me. He was about 6'3" and well over 270 pounds, which was enormous to me.

"Can I help you?" the man asked.

"I'm looking to get a membership," I said.

As he stood towering over me, he asked me a series of questions about my goals and tested my knowledge about lifting and form. Then he introduced himself.

"I am Pat, the owner."

"Hey, I'm Niall," I replied.

"Let me show you the gym," he said.

"Sure!"

We walked toward the treadmills that ran along the right side of the gym and he pointed out the equipment in the gym. As I looked around, I saw that the equipment was outdated. He noticed that I was looking at the condition of the equipment and let me know that everything was maintained and kept in good working condition. He actually performed the maintenance himself. It was only one big space with no dividing walls except for where the bathrooms were. It was a serious gym and I was serious about weight lifting.

There was an area in the gym called the "Pit" where all the serious lifters liked to train. I eventually worked my way into this area and got to know the lifters there. They were much larger than the rest of the gym members and they had the most experience. I asked them many questions and gained a lot of knowledge. I learned all the fundamentals of how to lift weights like breathing and form, how to control the weight, the benefits of lifting heavy with low reps, and the benefits of lifting light weights with high reps. Each style of lifting has its own advantages. They also taught me the details of hand placement and grip for the exercises, which also play a factor in what muscles are hit.

I gained so much experience from working out in Pat's Iron Works Gym. One day, I saw a picture on the wall of Pat in peak shape. His pose was just like the picture of my instructor in my art class at high school. It was a stunning photo. He was posed at a slight side profile while he held a muscle pose with one arm flexed. Pat has many accomplishments in bodybuilding, including a world title in powerlifting. Whenever he shared knowledge about working out, I listened. Works felt like home for me because of its atmosphere. The sound of steel clanking and AC/DC blasting always got me into my zone.

After Iron Works, I tried out several other gyms. The next gym had newer equipment, but the environment didn't suit my lifting style. The weights were different, and nothing seemed to feel right. The next gym had equipment similar to Iron Works, which was the type of equipment that I liked. There were a few guys that I recognized from other gyms I had attended, which showed me that I wasn't the only one who was trying out what other gyms had to offer. Since this new gym was across the city from my home, it was hard to get to. I ended up leaving and returning to the place that I enjoyed the most, where I got my best gains — Iron Works Gym.

At the time of my return to Iron Works, I was training for my modelling career and my body was transforming due to my weight lifting efforts. I was seventeen and specifically preparing for a photoshoot which would help get me into a modelling convention in Vancouver. It was great to walk back into the gym and know that I was able to work out in the atmosphere I enjoyed the most. I was able to get back to business. There was something soothing about working out at Iron Works — it was an environment where I was most focused and determined.

16

MODELLING

One day towards the end of Grade 10, my friend, Dan, and I were walking in the mall when a woman approached us. She was the owner and operator of a well-known modelling agency in Saskatoon. Neither of us was aware that there was an amateur fashion show in the mall later that day. We were surprised when she asked us if we would like to participate. I had sudden feelings of excitement and doubt. Here was a woman trying to convince me to walk on a runway in front of spectators and judges!

The top three amateurs picked in the show had the potential to work with the agency. Linda, the owner of the agency, assured me that it would be a fun experience and reassured me that I had nothing to lose and potentially everything to gain. I agreed to do the show, and she quickly let me know the times and showed me the outfits that I would wear. I went for some quick fittings from some of the stores that were in the mall. After the fittings, I went to the men's changing area. This was where it really sank in for me; I was so nervous. I had never pictured myself as a model but I trusted her judgment since she was a professional. Suddenly, a feeling of confidence came over me.

It could be argued that she was just looking for people to participate in the show, or she saw a look that she liked. Either way, I was in the show, and I accepted the fact that the judges would pick the best of the participants that showed up that day.

While I was backstage putting on my first outfit, I thought about the fact that I did not know anything about walking on a runway, whatsoever. I had seen some runway shows on TV though, and from what I gathered, a model would walk straight down the runway and stop, allowing people to have a look. Then they would do a turn and walk back and turn again. That is all I knew at the time. Linda came back to the changing area and let us know to make eye contact with the crowd and to be sure to look at the judges and smile. She also reminded us that the crowd was here for us and that we should have fun! It was impeccable timing on her part; I felt I now had some direction on what to do and what the judges were looking for.

There were many groups of models ahead of us, with children, teen boys, and girls alternating. They all had their turn on the stage. It was soon our turn, the teen boy group, and someone came to the changing area to tell us to be ready!

As our names were called, we lined up in the order we would appear on stage. I was ninth in line, which allowed me to watch the other eight models before me from a crack in the curtain. We were told not to peek! They said it would move the curtains and draw attention from the audience. I couldn't help myself and neither could the other competitors. One by one, the guys were called on stage. My heart was pounding, and I took deep breaths to calm my nervousness.

Finally, my name was called, and I was sent out to the stage. It was not a big stage, but I walked corner to corner and then in front of the judges. I had a huge smile while making eye contact with everyone at the table. Three of the five judges were looking down at the paper in front of them and writing things down. In my head, I was thinking, Wow, that was a fast decision. But really, I had no clue what they were writing.

I remember trying to take my time on the stage. Later Linda told us that all the models rushed a bit—maybe we were all a bit nervous. When I was walking back to exit the stage, I took one last look into the crowd and gave one more smile for good measure. I remember feeling relieved as I started walking behind the dividers, which separated the models from the stage.

I waited patiently for the results. Who would the top three guys be from my group? I felt that there were only two other guys that would be my contenders: Dan and another fellow who was a good looking and built individual. As we all hung up our outfits, Linda was handed the results and she came back to our area to let us know who the winners were. I took second place! I came second behind the built guy, and Dan took third. Linda handed me an envelope and inside was a certificate for $400, which could be used towards joining her modelling agency.

I was pleased with my placement in the competition. I was happy that I even placed. When Linda handed me the envelope, she looked happy, and she explained a bit about what the certificate could be used for. She said that I should think about coming into the agency and discussing what my next steps could be. She suggested that I use the certificate toward a modelling course which could give me the necessary skills to be a model, like how to walk the runway.

I took her up on her offer and attended a meeting where she went over the course outline and let me know what would be taught and about the instructors at her agency. It sounded good, so I signed up for the course. My parents signed off as they were legal guardian; they were happy that the $400 covered the full price of the training.

The course taught me the knowledge and necessary skills to succeed on the runway and in the industry. I was hooked. The more I learned, the more my interest grew. I became focused, and it wasn't long into the course before I developed a real passion for modelling. We also learned about how models care for themselves, like how to take care of our skin and hygiene. I was like a sponge in my need to learn more.

It wasn't too long before I got a call from Linda; she let me know about several fashion galas that were in the works. I did two shows for her for free. When she signed me up as a model, we had agreed that I would get some experience by doing the free shows, so it was worth it. I felt that I needed to master the runway. I practiced my turns in the basement hallway of my parent's house. I made it a goal that I would practice turns until they were absolutely perfect. Half turns, quarter turns, walkarounds (which were my favorite), and walk backs were all turns that allowed me to work with any type of choreography at a show.

Linda taught me so much. She was particular about how the models represented her shows. If it wasn't the way she envisioned, we would continue to work on it until she was happy. Sometimes it would only take three full rehearsals, but there were times when it took many tries to get it right. There were also times when, no matter how much we rehearsed, we just didn't get it right. We were told that we had to show up early the next morning and get back on the runway until it was perfect. At times it was frustrating when I was not the one messing up, to sit and watch other models until they got it right. But that was all part of the industry, and I never complained about it. I really loved watching a show come together. There was a huge energy in knowing that the next time you stepped out on the stage, there was an audience and all eyes would be on you.

On the eve of any show, I would make sure that all my body details were taken care of. I cut my nails, filed them, and then nicely buffed them. I had a bit of a baby face when I started to model, so I really didn't have to shave. I would use a mask on my face the night before to keep my skin looking fresh, and I would groom and shape my eyebrows, making sure that they were symmetrical.

It always excited me to get a call from the agency. It was a simple process: I would get a call and from there I made sure that I was available for the dates that were needed for rehearsals and fittings. I really enjoyed going to fittings. I saw it as an opportunity to meet the company that I had the privilege of representing on stage. Upon entering a store, I'd smile and introduce myself. I always gave a firm handshake and made eye contact. It was a nice ice breaker when a client saw a smile. I loved the creative process of the fittings because I was allowed to try on a few outfits they had in mind and see what worked for my size and build. When the outfits were picked, they were always hung and wrapped in garment bags and labeled with my name. After I left a store, I would always go home and start practicing my steps and spend some time smiling in the mirror and experimenting with different angles while paying attention to the lighting and seeing how shadows would hit my face.

From the moment I was first asked to participate in a fashion gala, I made sure that when I walked out on stage, I was at my very best. This really helped with my confidence. I knew that if I showed up feeling great, my positivity would transfer to the runway. These skills were all taught as words of advice from Linda. She had a stern way of letting you know what to do but delivered it in a manner that immediately clicked in my head. No matter whether the fashion show was in a mall or an auditorium, the seriousness and professionalism of the industry were always real. I needed to take everything seriously and at the same time find the joy in it. I always had fun at these types of fashion galas. They were great opportunities to mingle with other models who were all chasing the same dreams and had the same ambition to work on their modelling careers.

With Linda's modelling agency, I gained a lot of experience. I learned runway modelling, mannequin modelling, catalog, and print modelling, and I worked with well-known professional photographers that travelled from bigger cities like Toronto and Vancouver. I had the opportunity to do outdoor shoots as well as studio photo shoots. A model doesn't just step in front of a camera and suddenly look great. It takes work and a lot of it.

When it came to doing an outdoor photoshoot, my mindset was similar to the mindset I had in preparing for a runway show. I knew the details were going to be a little more extreme as the camera shots would be closer up and more personal. I didn't prepare for a shoot in the few days before it. I started prepping two to three weeks in advance. I made sure to drink lots of water and used facial scrubs and skin creams to make sure that my skin had a healthy glow and was clear of blemishes. I paid attention to my skin, and if it became oily, I was sure to dab a napkin on the oily spot to avoid the pore to create a blackhead. I used blackhead remover strips two days before an outdoor shoot and allowed my pores to shrink down by using freezing water, which would tighten my skin. By diminishing the size of the pores, I was maximizing the potential of my skin and making sure it looked even and smooth.

On the eve of a shoot, I would place eight spoons in the refrigerator and apply the models' secret — Preparation H — under and around my eyes to take away puffiness from my eyes and firm the skin up so it was tight in the morning. You are probably wondering what the spoons are for. On the day of a shoot, I took the spoons out, one pair at a time, and placed the rounded sides of the spoons on my eyes and around the sockets of my eyes. I would hold the spoons on my eyelids as long as I could until the cold turned warm, and then wait five minutes or so and repeat until all the spoons were used. This brightened up my eyes and allowed me to smile with them for the shoot. Yes, you read that correctly. A person can smile with their eyes. It is an exceptional skill which I found helpful during photo shoots.

I was enjoying my experience and knowledge provided in the modelling world. But my life was about to be rocked.

17

HITTING THE POST

My friend, Marcus, introduced me to his friend, Lincoln. Marcus and Lincoln shared another friend — Andrew — who had an older blue Trans-Am. Andrew had put a lot of work into the car, making it powerful and incredibly fast. Andrew loved driving it, and Marcus and Andrew used to pick me up, and we would go cruise around. I enjoyed riding in the car because it was tuned up for speed, and I liked anything that went fast. One day, Lincoln pulled up in the car, alone. Lincoln told me Andrew was out of town and had said he could use the vehicle while he was away. Lincoln and I went to pick up Marcus.

The three of us were heading to Lincoln's house, following Melissa, Lincoln's girlfriend. She had an errand to make at the mall and we were following her. Then we would all be heading to Lincoln's. When we came up to the lights, the light was green. Lincoln didn't proceed through the light; instead, he allowed the traffic that had already cleared the light get further away, including Melissa's car.

I could hear the engine get louder and louder. Lincoln had his foot on the break and on the gas at the same time. The engine's RPMs were getting very high. The traffic light turned yellow and then red, and suddenly Lincoln removed his foot off the brake. I sunk back into my seat. The tires were spinning and the car was accelerating very quickly—faster than I have felt any other vehicle accelerate. I looked ahead into the traffic; the cars seemed to be far enough away that we were not in any immediate danger. Then I noticed the traffic had stopped and there was a car turning ahead of us into the mall. Our car continued to speed toward the stopped traffic. I could hear the engine was working very hard. Lincoln had the pedal to the floor. I looked over at him and saw him grab the steering wheel more aggressively. I couldn't understand why he wasn't slowing down.

Then I realized he was trying to catch as much speed as he could in as short a distance as possible. I took a quick glance at the speedometer. It read 140 km/hour. We were still accelerating; Lincoln was not letting off the gas. I sat there terrified, unable to speak or scream. Finally, Lincoln removed his foot from the gas and slightly hit the brake pedal. The car pulled extremely hard to the left, putting us head-to-head with the vehicle that was coming our way. Because the traffic was stopped ahead of us, Melissa was stopped right ahead of us.

We were still travelling at a fast rate when Lincoln veered to the right to avoid smashing head-on into the oncoming car. He wrestled the car back into our lane, but his girlfriend was stopped directly in front of us. We were still travelling over 100 km/hour. Lincoln steered the car right to avoid rear-ending her. Out of control, we jumped the curb. Ahead of us were trees and apartments. Lincoln avoided them and came back to the street. Still out of control. About to slam into the back of Melissa's car. Lincoln's final attempt to avoid her steered us right into a lamp post.

When we hit the post, the car went from 80 km/hour to a dead stop. Not wearing a seatbelt, Marcus slammed into the back of my seat. It was like a bomb had gone off in my back, exploding shrapnel everywhere.

Immediately after the accident, I remember a moment when everything was still. The light at the top of the lamp post had fallen onto the car and bounced off of the vehicle and onto the sidewalk. The floor was pushed up under where my feet were and the engine of the car was right in front of me. Lincoln was pinched and pressed against the steering wheel, which was folded over and had snapped apart in one place.

The first thing I heard after the impact was Lincoln yelling. I couldn't understand him at first, but then his voice became clearer and more precise. He kept repeating, "Are you guys okay? Are you guys okay? Talk to me."

I am not sure if I said anything. I just sat there in my seat, not moving and not knowing what type of injuries I had sustained. I thought I had broken my back.

There was no response from Marcus in the back seat except for a series of moans. He was turned upside down in the back seat. The back of my seat had a solid plastic backing and when his face hit the back of my seat, it left an imprint of his profile in the backing.

All I wanted to do was to get out of the vehicle. My window was down, and I knew I was okay, enough to think that I should exit the car. I remember placing one foot down and then the other foot. I took a few steps and collapsed onto the street.

I lay there for a while, thinking: Wow, thank God, I am alive.

A bystander came to help me off of the street and sat me on the curb.

This accident caused intense fear in my family as they compared it to the accident that had taken my brother's life less than a year earlier. They feared for my safety. I could have lost my life.

18

CALGARY AND BACK

My life was spiraling more out of control than I would admit. It became evident to my parents as well and they reached out to my cousin John for help. A plan was formulated, making him my legal guardian, which would allow me to attend school in Alberta where John was attending college. I was enrolled in high school in southwest Calgary.

Although my cousin was persistent in keeping me on track, little did I realize that he was still in pain from the loss of my brother. He was taking steroids during the time I was staying with him.

One evening, he pulled out a small glass vial and a syringe, and he asked me, "Do you know what this is?"

"No," I replied.

We didn't discuss the subject again. I did later learn that whatever it was that he had been taking gave him a horrible temper. On top of the hurt of losing my brother, who was his best friend and favorite cousin, it could not have been easy on him being responsible for me. I believe his intentions were good, but he didn't know how to care for me in the way I needed to be cared for during the grieving process of losing my big brother. How could he? He still had his brother, and I didn't.

Just like back in Saskatoon, I met new people and made new friends. I remember having a crush on a girl, Natalie, who was blonde and incredibly attractive. She had full lips and was in great shape. She dressed well, and we hung out quite often. I learned that she liked to party, drink, and get crazy on weekends. I began to feel that same rush that I had felt before. Not only was I crushing on Natalie, but we had something in common — cocaine and alcohol. At the time, I was working at a fast-food chain just down the street from my school. Apart from paying John rent for staying at his house, I had no other bills. Natalie and I would go to social outings together, and we both became popular in the school as our group continued to grow. We had a tight-knit crew of what I called "the good-looking club."

Natalie would eventually become my girlfriend, and we often were the people that brought the energy to a party. We loved to chat and talk about deep thoughts with others when we did cocaine. I really enjoyed that aspect of what the drug did for me because I felt real. I didn't have to be a fake person. I would just say things as they were. I found that other people liked that about me too, and even though I was using drugs, I wasn't judged by many, as they could see the good in me and not the negatives.

As my social life grew in Calgary, so did my cousin's temper. I used to fall asleep to mellow and slow music. One morning, I woke up, and John was in my face yelling at me. He was livid. I can't think of what set him off, but he was so mad that he threw my CD player against the wall. It didn't break and still worked, but this put a fear in me that I wasn't willing to deal with.

The incident with John yelling at me and throwing my CD player against the wall triggered something deep within me. Memories that had been suppressed deep in my brain now came floating to the surface. I remembered the sexual abuse that took place when I was a kid. It all became clear as day. I was only seventeen years and the tormenting thoughts that arose in my head brought huge fears.

I knew I had to get out of that situation. I quickly formulated a plan to escape from his violence and get back to Saskatoon as fast as possible. I had a job, all I had to do was wait until I was paid, and I would buy a bus ticket and hit the road. I wasn't even going to tell John; I would just disappear. I was going to tell my work though and my school. I just told them things were not going as planned and I had to return to Saskatoon. Everyone was very understanding, and my plan was executed.

In the end though, I did tell John. I told him that how he yelled at me was unacceptable and that I would be leaving. I thanked him for his efforts to help me out, and that was all. He even drove me to the bus station.

19

THE CHINESE FIGHT

Back in Saskatoon, I gave school yet another chance. It was a new fresh start. I had been working as a cook at a fast-food restaurant in Calgary and I applied to transfer to their location in Saskatoon. It was close to home and was right across the street from the high school which my brother and many of my friends had attended. By the time I returned, they had all graduated. I had dropped out two times by that point, and I struggled with my education and struggled with myself as an individual.

It didn't take long before I had found all my old hookups for drugs and my old party buddies. They seemed to pop out from every corner. There was always a big party coming up, or someone would say, "Let's go grab a beer," and one beer would always turn into ten and by the sixth beer, we were already looking for cocaine. It never took much, just a simple suggestion, and we would be looking. It was like clockwork. Broadway Avenue was always filled with people who knew where to get the drugs we needed.

I would bump into friends along the way. Some lived in apartments above bars. These places were dives. Typically, I would never be seen partying in such a place, but I had friends who lived in these places, and they hung around people who I enjoyed. Who was I to judge these people? I was doing no better than they were. Although I was living with my parents and had a nicer place to rest my head, we were the same type of people. I was a druggie and an addict just like them. I was someone who enjoyed parties and got ripped roaring drunk until all hours of the night.

One Saturday night, some friends and I thought it would be great if we all did a couple of hits of LSD and then went to watch a friend of ours sing at a little Chinese lounge in Saskatoon. It was wintertime and there was a fresh blanket of snow on the ground. I can remember not having jackets on; we were so high that we couldn't feel the cold. It was around -20°C. About ten of us piled into this little lounge to watch our friend sing. She was an incredibly talented singer, so we would support her any chance we could. There were about twenty people in the place, tops. We started to have drinks, and we were all having a good time, and then it happened.

I believe it was my friend Kevin who insulted the waitress, saying that she had ripped him off or short-changed him or something. (I am not 100% sure, but if my memory serves me right, it was Kevin who began the incident.) He started making a big deal out of it, and things escalated quickly.

Soon a guy from another table piped in, yelling at Kevin. We all had Kevin's back — that was just the way we rolled back then. The punches started flying, tables tipped over, and glasses broke. It was a full-on bar fight.

Soon, the whole place was filled with Chinese people. Some held meat cleavers or forty-ounce bottles of booze which, by the way, can crack your skull right open and slice you up in a big way. We were unaware that there was a backroom to this place where there was illegal gambling. More than one hundred people piled out from the back. They were all holding weapons and were ready to kill if needed. It was ten against one hundred. It was so crammed that we weren't able to throw a punch. We were pushed to the back of the lounge against the wall. We were cornered and staring at a large crowd of people who wanted to hurt us. It probably wasn't smart to mess with the Chinese mafia.

After talking for a bit, everyone settled down, and a narrow path started to open towards the front door. They were giving us a chance to leave, pretty much unharmed and breathing, which I thought was terrific because someone could easily have been killed. I remember thanking them on the way out. We all did because we all knew it could have been much worse.

After we were all out of the lounge, we hit the streets of Saskatoon, running around and sliding in the fresh blanket of snow. I only remember this because the roads looked like they were made out of diamonds that were sparkling and twinkling blue, red, purple, and orange; it was amazing, and we soon forgot how dangerous a situation we had just been in. We laughed it off. We continued with our night, having more laughs and good times.

20

THE ACID FLASHBACK

Dan and I had taken a trip to Calgary to see a friend, Melania. I had met Melania in high school when I lived in Calgary with my cousin. We drove to Calgary in Dan's car. It was a small white car, but he had put an expensive stereo in it, and it thumped. The bass shook the bolts loose off the license plate. When we arrived at Melania's parents' house, we chilled out, ate, chatted, and caught up. It was nice. The next night we had planned to get some booze and head over to a friend of Melania's.

Then it happened. Dan asked Melania if she knew of any place we could find some acid. She knew a lot of people, so she started calling friend after friend, on the hunt. She finally found someone, but we had to drive to pick it up. We all piled into the car, and away we went.

After meeting up to buy the acid, we returned to Melania's friends home. We all took some tabs. Let the fun times begin, right? Wrong. At first, things were going well. We were watching the movie "The Mask," featuring Jim Carrey. We were full of laughs, and everyone was having fun; until I had to go into the washroom. That is when my night went downhill—rapidly.

I was in the bathroom and suddenly an intense vision started.

The sound of a vehicle roaring down a highway came to my thoughts. I could see it; the headlights were rectangular and the car was traveling at a high speed. I could hear the sound of the engine revving at a high RPM. I could see the vehicle was out of control, the driver hitting the brakes, the tires screeching. I couldn't make out the driver's face because it was dark. Suddenly a smash, the sound of metal crushing, metal glass breaking and everything went into slow motion.

My view switched to being in the vehicle that was hit by the out-of-control car. I could see the front seat passenger in clear sight. It as Cyril. It was as if I was looking at the accident through his eyes as he experienced it. Everything was in slow motion. I could see the glass piercing his face, leaving small cuts, and his body moving from the impact. The car was airborne, and I could hear the vehicle smashing as it landed on its roof.

I yelled out in pain, screaming in pain, crying. I had totally lost it. In an outburst of suppressed grief, I had envisioned a re-enactment of my brother's death. I had witnessed my brother's death. Even though I had not been there and it was three years later, it seemed real to me. I curled up in a ball on the bathroom floor and cried out in pain.

21

SCHOOL AND BAD FRIENDS

Since I had dropped out of school twice and didn't have my high school diploma, there was always something in the back of my head that directed me back to school. I remember staying sober long enough to talk with my mom and ask her for her thoughts on the idea of my going back to school. She wasn't opposed to the idea, but she made it very clear that she didn't want to waste money on buying school books and notebooks if I was going to drop out. I felt like a failure, not as good as the rest of my friends that had stuck it out and graduated. I was way behind my fellow students, but I decided I would give education another try.

But I soon fell into the drugs and party scene. School was just not important enough to me. I skipped classes and hung out with people and did drugs. I would leave school to get wasted. I was kicked out of my high school and sent to another one, where many other students that were struggling with the same problems were sent. I knew people there, and not just a few. They were all pretty bad people who had fought for gangs. If they were not related to a gang, they sure loved the gang life. They were not the kind of people anyone dared to mess with. They were connected, and it was well known that we would inflict pain onto those that crossed us. And now, I was one of them.

I can remember being the garage of one of my new friends, drinking and doing rips of cocaine, when a fellow brother came running in saying he saw someone walking down the alley that had crossed our group or jumped one of us before. Everyone rushed out of the garage and into the alley. There the guy was, calling us out and name-calling. He said something I would never dare say. He said, "You bunch of niggers." Well, that was the turning point of the exchange.

Terry walked toward the guy, and the fight started. Now, there is a code to such a fight, which is, no one jumps in unless the fight is over and the winner keeps beating on the loser when they are down and can't defend themselves. That was the code we lived by anyway. Well, as the fight continued, they tussled and rolled around while exchanging punches. Terry finally got the best of the exchange and landed more punches. He had him beat and left him in the middle of the alley. It was done, and Terry was victorious. Or so we thought.

All of a sudden, the guy got up and pulled a knife and charged at Terry. We all went into protective mode, and it wasn't long before this guy with a knife was getting kicked and stomped on by many of us. Well, as you would expect, the situation only got worse from there. After a knife, always comes a gun.

The guy, who was just beat, knew people with guns, and the people who would use them, as did we. We knew he would be coming back, with a gun, and with friends with guns. So, we went into defense mode. People in our group were armed and ready to rock.

I remember my buddy saying, "Niall you better split, bro. You don't need to get involved in this. This isn't your war."

I was filled with adrenaline and very cautious when I left the area. I was on foot, high on cocaine, and a little inebriated. I knew that friends of the guy who was just been beaten would be on their way, guns blazing. From what I was later told of that night, no one was killed, but some were injured severely and hospitalized.

I was protected in some strange way. I never had a beef with anyone, mainly because I was smart enough not to cross people. I was friends with people from groups that didn't get along. I guess you could say I had friends on both sides of the fence. I never was a part of any organization, but I knew a lot of people, and I never had a problem when it came to them being able to trust me. I was a straight shooter. When I did mess up, I owned up to it. I never got beat down, but I was occasionally put in my place. Others around me would get "cuffed" or "bitch slapped" which is getting backhanded in the face. Others would get beaten and kicked around.

Sometimes the beatings would happen right in front of me while other times I was asked to leave the room. Either way, I never liked the feeling when I knew someone was going to get licked.

What was the leading cause for these beatings you may ask? It is really simple ... drugs, specifically cocaine. Marijuana, crack, ecstasy, you name it; it was all being moved by people I knew. I wasn't ever directly involved in the drug trade, but it surrounded me, and I always had drugs at my fingertips.

The runners or dealers would get beat because sometimes what they were given, and the amount they gave back, didn't match up. People were usually short because they were using the product themselves. Let's get real, if you use, you lose; it is very black and white. There is a saying, "Never get high on your own supply," which is also quoted in one of my favorite movies, "Scarface."

Not matching up meant they were short. A rough estimate of the cost of cocaine at that time was $60-$80 per gram, $150-$250 per Eightball (an eighth of an ounce, or three and a half grams). If someone wanted an ounce of cocaine, that ounce (28 grams) usually went for $1,600 to $1,900. But a clever dealer could make $2,800 if they sold the ounce by individual gram packages. So, you can see where the profit came in. If you sold enough ounces, in a short time, you would see your money grow and grow fast.

To make even more money, a dealer could start cutting the drugs, which would give the customers a crappier product, but the quality would be just good enough to keep them coming back. That is why I call it the "devil's drug."

22

PLAYING WHILE ON THE HOTEL JOB

My parents were less than impressed with my behavioral issues upon my return to Saskatoon. My mom gave me the ultimatum to move out or get a job. So, I started looking for new work. Dan's mom worked at a five-star hotel in downtown Saskatoon, and Dan was a cook there as well, so I figured maybe I could work there too. I applied for a job in the catering department and soon I was working as a porter. A porter was a person who helps set up banquet rooms for special events or meetings that occurred weekly with various business groups.

As a porter, I would help set the rooms up, placing the tablecloths on tables and setting up the staging and podiums. Next, another group would come in and set up the water glasses around the table. How they set the table depended upon the event, whether it was a wedding or conference or whatever. I remember that the food was one of the perks of the job. Whenever there was an event or a booking, the food was always to die for! I ate like a king! After the event was complete, we would gather in the kitchen and eat whatever we wanted and as much as we wanted. It was all pretty sweet.

The porters worked in teams, partnering with someone. I was often teamed up with a heavyset guy by the name of Dorian. He was a really nice guy and it was quite clear he was intellectually challenged. Being heavyset, he would sweat a lot when things got busy, often wiping the sweat from his face and forehead. I would sometimes stop the work and suggest that he get some water. I knew he was thirsty, so I sent him off for a short break.

When he came back, I would ask him, "How do you feel? Do you feel better, bud?"

"Yes," he would say, and then he got back to work with a happy look on his face.

Although he took many breaks, Dorian was a hard worker and was always pleasant to talk to while we worked. Because we worked nights, we were able to play music from the satellite stations in the different rooms we worked in. It was great that we both enjoyed the rock station, which often played some of my favorites like Guns N' Roses, Metallica, and Poison. We would rock out to them.

Because I always worked evenings, I never really got the chance to meet employees that worked during the day. One day, I came waltzing in much earlier than I needed to, and the woman at the front desk caught my eye. Her name was Mackenzie. There was a doorway that led downstairs between the front desk and the main elevators of the hotel. I needed to walk past her to get to the stairs. I remember looking over just before I entered the doorway and noticed her looking at me. Our eyes locked and a smile came across both our faces. I was always early for work after that day.

We started to chat when I walked by. Soon we began to spend time together, going for walks. My attraction to her was quite clear. She had an amazing French accent, beautiful clear skin, a fantastic smile, nice white teeth, and an athletic build. Around the time we started to get to know one another, the staff Christmas party was coming up, so I asked her if she would like to go with me. She said she was happy to. I can't say we dated, but we did spend a lot of time together, and things naturally progressed. Mackenzie was, by far, one of the most attractive women of all the staff.

At seventeen, I was much younger than her, and she brought up our age difference to me. One time, she asked if I was okay with the fact that she was twenty-four, and I was seventeen. I remember sitting in the hotel restaurant with her when she asked me the question. Obviously, my reply was that I was okay with it, but I asked her in return if she was okay with my age. She was, and so we agreed to see one another.

I remember telling my friend Paul and a few others how I was seeing this older lady at the time. It was all very exciting.

At the Christmas staff party, I think every single male employee hit on her, even when their wives were there. It was insane! I sat back, and for some reason, enjoyed the attention she was getting; all these men wanted her. She politely smiled and pointed over to me and asked me to come to her, and she introduced me as the man she was with. "This is Niall; he is my date."

Don't think for a second that I wasn't intimidated by these older guys, but I knew deep down that I had the upper hand since I was tall, dark, and handsome. Well, at least, that is how she described what she found attractive about me when we first starting hanging out. As the party continued, we had a lot of wine and apparently didn't hide the fact that we were physically attracted to one another. The next day at work, I was told that we were making out everywhere in the hotel, lip locked for anyone to see, including the security staff. It is safe to say that our connection was a topic of conversation for the other employees the following day.

As time went on, Mackenzie and I continued hanging out. One day she invited me over to her place. It was early afternoon, and I clearly remember walking into her building. We walked up the two flights of stairs to her apartment, and she casually mentioned that we would not have a lot of time.

We rushed to get into the apartment and get things started. We kissed as we entered the apartment and undressed while heading towards the couch. As both of our bodies hit the couch half-naked, I asked her, "What is the rush?"

She said her boyfriend would be home soon.

"WHAT?"

She told me not to worry and pulled me back in and started making out with me again. There was a real sudden rush that came over me. This was really exciting now for some reason. We continued kissing for a while, and she asked me if I wanted some wine or a beer.

She got up and then suddenly began to frantically run around and pick up clothes.

"You need to leave, right now!"

"Why? What's going on?" I asked.

"My boyfriend is home early!"

I frantically leaped up off of the couch like a kernel of corn that had just popped. I had my pants, shoes, and shirt in my arms, and I ran out of the door and toward the back entrance. I reached the back door of the building, and I jumped off the third stair from the bottom and hit the door just as I heard the door in the front of the building slam shut. It is possible that Mackenzie's boyfriend heard the same kind of sound as the door slammed behind me.

I ran down the back lane, in my boxers and my socks, holding tight to my shoes, shirt, and trousers. I finally stopped and took the time to get dressed.

The real kicker of this story was when I heard who her boyfriend was. He was the big brother of a friend of mine from high school. He was much larger than I was and had a reputation of being tough and was someone who could easily wipe the floor with someone my size. He could have put me in a world of hurt, I am sure. If I had known about Mackenzie's boyfriend, obviously I would not have gotten involved with her. You just don't do that.

At the moments while running down the alley, I felt a rush. I had gotten away clear and free. There were obviously other addictions than just drugs and alcohol that I faced.

The next time I saw Mackenzie, she said that it probably wasn't a good idea that we see each other anymore. In my head, I thought when she told me this: YOU THINK?!

We remained friends, but we both knew what type of danger we were playing with. We talked once in a while at work when we could, but then Mackenzie moved away from Saskatoon, which removed all temptation.

I wasn't with the hotel for much longer after she left. The main reason for my departure was my supervisor's attitude. He was a guy who thought he was much cooler than he really was, walking around like he was every woman's dream man with his nose in the air. His demeanor made me sick. He flirted with all the girls and always tried to pick them up. It was around this time that I realized that arrogance gets you nowhere. I always like to believe that I was, for the most part, humble and polite. That may not always have been a good thing, but that was me.

23

UNCONSCIOUS FOR ALL
THE RIGHT REASON

One of my next jobs was working as a landscaper for a large company. We planted trees all over the city, which was labor intensive. But at least I was working outside in the sun while others were stuck inside. I tried out this type of employment because my buddy Marcus had been working at it for a while and found that he loved it. I thought I would give it a shot and I'm glad I did. It is great to see your hard work manifest into something that will most likely be around forever. Working in this job, I quickly felt the joy Marcus described to me. There was something about the physical aspect and demand of the job that was great. I really enjoyed the shoveling part for some reason, which others didn't. I was always willing to pick up the shovel and push myself into moving any pile of dirt or mulch.

One particular job comes to mind. It was in the Exhibition grounds a few blocks away from my parents' house. These were the same Exhibition grounds where my brother had BMX-raced back in the day. This area had been neglected for years after the City of Saskatoon had moved the BMX track to the opposite corner of the grounds. The company I was working for was awarded the contract to fix the area up and make it look presentable. That is exactly what we did.

We brought in the bobcats and big trucks full of dirt and mulch and got to work. We planted new trees and shrubs and followed the layout of the new plans for the area. Now, I haven't told too many people this story, mostly because it was ridiculous. It was on this job that I knocked myself clean out.

After we planted a tree, we would pound steel posts next to the tree to support it. I would place a post to the right of the tree and pound the post into the ground with a post pounder. A post pounder is shaped like a cylinder and is about four inches in circumference. Made of solid steel, it is about three feet long and has handles on both sides. Eighteen inches or so is hollowed out, which allows it to slide over the post that you are pounding into the ground. The rest is solid steel, so the weight of this tool makes it able to hit these posts into the ground. Given that I was always looking for a physical job, I took on this job to pound all these posts into the ground and then tie wire around the posts and trees. By the third tree, I felt that I had caught on quite well. Although it was heavy and physical work, I quite enjoyed it.

The whole unit weighed between 35-40 pounds. The posts were seven feet in length, and I was 5'10", so I would get the post into the ground a bit and start hitting it with the post pounder, pounding it lower and lower into the ground until only about four feet were showing.

When I knocked myself out, I came to clear the post (which means to go high with the post pounder), and when I started coming down, I caught the edge of the post. I was still pulling down though, and I pulled the solid steel part, the post pounder, right down on the top of my head. The sun disappeared, and before I knew it, I was sleeping like a baby.

I woke up alone. I was laying in the grass with the post pounder not too far from my hand, and my hat was off my head. I remember I tried to get up and act as if nothing had happened. Thank goodness there was no one else that saw what I had done—mainly because my supervisor on the job had just told me to be careful with the post pounder. I was a lot more cautious pounding the posts after that; there was a lesson learned there, not only about safety but also that I could break free from addictions and have a real life, if only for short periods of time.

24

HELLO CRYSTAL METH

My drug use took another turn when I began experimenting with Crystal Meth. A friend who I often used drugs with throughout the years, Damian, knowing my desires for various substances, came up to me one day and said to me, "Niall, you think cocaine is good, you should check this shit out."

He pulled out a glass tube with a round ball at the end. He pulled out a small container which held little crystals and tapped a few of these small crystals through a small hole into the rounded part of the glass pipe. I remember he was careful not to drop any of, what seemed to be, very precious shards of crystals. He pulled out a lighter and heated the ball of the pipe, rotating it back and forth while explaining to me what he was doing.

"See it melting?" he asked.

"Yeah," I replied. As he turned the pipe back and forth, I could see a brownish puddle forming. I took the pipe, mimicking what he did previously.

I handed the pipe back to Damion.

"Watch this," he said.

He put his lips to the tube of the pipe and slowly inhaled, sucking slowly and steadily. He kept turning the pipe side to side until his lungs were full. He exhaled, and a massive cloud of smoke came out.

"You want to try it?"

I was nervous but excited at the same time.

"Yeah man, hook me up!"

He needed a moment to gain his bearings. He was already super high. Once he was okay, he started the same process and shook some shards into the pipe again. I noticed he had not put as many as he had put in his pipe, so I called him on it.

"Hey, why are you not putting as much for me as you did for yourself?"

"Trust me, Niall. You don't need a lot."

So, he started the process again, and he burned it and turned it, just like he did for himself.

"Are you ready?" he asked.

"Yep," I replied and proceeded to put my lips to the pipe.

"Okay, suck slowly."

Maxing out my lung capacity, I inhaled as much as I could. I quickly exhaled since Damian had told me not to hold it in. The result was the same; a huge cloud of smoke came from my mouth.

I was high instantly. This high was different, and I was excited to have another hit. Meth gave me a rush like no other. The high came faster, and the effects lasted for a decent amount of time.

Momentarily, meth quickly became my drug of choice. It was cheaper than cocaine and I could get just as high. Later, after learning how it was made, it all came to a screeching halt. When I learned about its effects on my brain and my body, I decided it just wasn't worth it.

So, I went back to cocaine.

25

ANOTHER ACCIDENT, ANOTHER TRAUMA

One day, my friend Dan and I decided to rent a movie. This decision resulted in a major car accident and for me, considerable physical trauma.

Dan and I were driving his girlfriend Emma's truck at the time. When we left the mall's parking lot after renting the movie, we drove down a main street, slowly approaching an avenue which was a cross street with a four-way stop.

When we come up to the stop sign, we made a complete stop. I looked right and then left and then right again and didn't see any cars. Dan proceeded into the intersection.

What we weren't expecting was a car travelling down the avenue at eighty kilometers an hour and running the stop sign. I didn't have time to see the car, I just caught a glimpse of the headlights right before impact.

The car smashed into the truck door right behind where I sat. I instantly felt the truck go airborne. The rear of the truck was off the ground, rotating and swinging around to the left. The violent impact jarred my entire body. The truck spun on its front wheels for two full rotations before coming to a stop. At the moment of impact, we were in the middle of the intersection, and by the time we landed, we were well onto the boulevard which separated the two-way street. Then we bounced back onto the road and landed in front of the first house on the block. The cab had separated from the remainder of the truck, landing over sixty feet away from where the rest truck came to a final stop.

A witness called for the police and Dan and I waited for them to arrive along with a tow truck.

Although I was in shock, I knew that this accident had done some real damage to me. I couldn't feel the pain at the time, but in the days that followed, I lost my ability to walk without extreme pain. I had herniated two discs in my back and they were bulging, pinching, and rubbing on my nerve. I became bedridden, tied to oxycodone, morphine, and other muscle relaxers. I couldn't work, I couldn't play sports, and I couldn't put on my socks by myself. Everything that I had been able to do before and had taken for granted was gone.

My life would never the same and for many years I would struggle with intense back pain. But I kept persevering. With the help of physiotherapy and putting to use my own weight training knowledge, I managed to be able to stand and walk.

26

ALMOST SAVED

One day my mother asked me if I would attend a Church service with her. I had long since given up on church, but I wanted to make my mom happy, so I agreed to go. My friends, Dan and Miles, agreed to come with us.

This is when things started to change.

I listened as the pastor spoke of an opportunity to clear myself from the painful sins that I had committed with the possibility of being forgiven. As I sat there listening, I was thinking to myself: Was this true? The pastor repeatedly expressed that if there was anyone who wanted to be baptized, in the name of Jesus, they should come forward. I pondered this and made a split decision. I stood up and raised my arms so that everyone could see that I needed the healing of Jesus. A man touched me on the shoulder and directed me where to go. I had no idea what was happening, but I headed toward the pool of water that was at the front of the congregation.

As I stood waiting for my turn, I started to have mixed emotions. I questioned myself, thinking: Do I really want to do this? Thoughts of childhood taunts came into my head. Would I be called a "Bible Thumper? But self-doubt left me as I felt the new energy of those that went before me. Each person that walked by me seemed changed, and I felt revitalized!

Finally, it was my turn. I walked out onto the platform, walked into the warm water, and stood waist deep waiting anxiously for what was to come. The pastor wasted no time and started praying in the name of Jesus Christ. He asked Jesus to put his blessing on me and to erase the sin in my heart and soul. The pastor fully submerged me into the water. Under the water, I felt in complete awe. I was different, changed. I was cleansed pure and felt joy consume my heart. It is unexplainable, but I knew I was forgiven in God's eyes after doing so much wrong. The hatred and pain were gone.

The thing is, this feeling didn't last, as much as I wished it would have. I have come to realize that after such a blessing, you have to keep up with the teachings and read and learn the word to keep — what's called the "Armor of God" — on. I did none of this. I wasn't swearing and doing all the bad things I was doing before, but again, the sins of the devil soon slipped back into my life, penetrating my soul with the devil's darts. Sin and lust consumed me; although, this time, it was much worse.

That old familiar feeling of emptiness and pain returned. I was so far gone that I saw no point in trying to climb out of the deep pit of sins that I was in. I could see the pain and disappointment all around me. I tried to hide my feelings from my family and my friends. I struggled with sin, and nothing good could come from this. The emptiness continued to grow. I couldn't look the people who actually loved me in the eye. I ran from the problems I had in my life and soon I didn't care about anyone or anything.

No one would have known; I was great at camouflaging the emptiness. On the outside, I looked as if I had it together, but in reality, I was crumbling. I was so wrapped up in drugs and other harsh sins of the world that I found myself fighting a battle I could not win, and I know that I inflicted pain on others.

Humans are always going to sin, that's just life, but there are ways through prayers that heal us along the way and allow us to help others and do good in the world. There were small glimpses of hope, but I chose to turn away from these. Addiction had such a firm grasp on my life, I just accepted the fact that I had to live with it.

I wanted to die.

The pain was so intense that the thought of killing myself became to feel like a real option. I pondered ways I could accomplish this. I took a mixture of uppers and downers, wishing that an overdose would end my pain. I pushed my limits to the max. Based on the amount of drugs I was doing, I should have died. I have heard stories of people overdosing doing less.

I no longer cared about my life. I thought of driving my car into a semi or off of a bridge. I started to get creative in my planning and went to dark places in my mind.

I was so close to completing the deed that I actually pulled my mom aside and confided in her that I was continuously contemplating suicide. As my mom listened to my words, I could feel her heart sink. I broke down in shame of my deceitfulness. It was the only time since the passing of my brother that I shed tears. My mother reached out and hugged me tight with both arms, and I buried my face in her shoulder, crying. She was loving and calm and requested a promise from me. She made me promise that I would never think these horrible thoughts again and that she would be the first person I would tell if they ever came back. How could I have thought that she didn't love me? I was mistaken, and I am forever grateful for my mother's love.

Now in saying all that, I didn't necessarily stop living the way I did, but I no longer viewed suicide as a real option.

Over the years, I have experienced many things that, in my eyes, should have "got the job done." I am referring to ending of my life. I have experienced car accidents that should have killed me. I put myself in harm's way with the activities I involved myself in and the people I associated with. I still do not even know, right now, how I am sitting here writing this book, other than I was protected under God's hand and that I have a purpose to fulfill.

Soon after this experience of sharing my suicide thoughts with my mother, a door opened for me.

27

AN OPPORTUNITY
AND A DECISION

Linda, the modelling agent Linda, called me and asked me to come down to her agency. When I arrived, she pulled me into her office and told me about an upcoming opportunity she believed I would do well at. The opportunity was a modelling convention in Vancouver, which was called Faces West. Linda explained to me that this was a huge opportunity where sixty-five of the world's top agencies came to meet and look at potential models from all over Canada.

I had roughly six months to prepare for this event. I was given a checklist of all the things I needed to get ready so that I was prepared to stand in front of the fashion agents. The right wardrobe was one of the things on the checklist. I needed a robe and various outfits that complimented my physique. I bought some tight CK briefs to wear for the underwear part of the show, which was required so that the agents could get a good look at model body types.

I was in the early stages of weight training, but Linda told me that I should not be too built. It was better to be slim and toned.

Most evenings, I jogged a 5.3 kilometer route and used the gym at school every day after school.

I did everything in my power to be prepared for this opportunity in Vancouver. Sixty-five of the top agencies would be there and was my big chance to see if I really had what it took to be in the modelling industry.

During this time, I began a relationship with a woman who was six years older than I. She was twenty-five and I was nineteen. She was very supportive of my efforts and helped me with my clothing choices for the convention. She even helped me out with the costs involved with the convention, which I am forever grateful for.

Although we only dated for six months, we experienced something that impacted our lives. She got pregnant a few weeks before I was to leave for Vancouver. We did not dare tell anyone. It was clear that we were not anywhere near ready to bring a child into the world. We were terrified. She decided to have an abortion, and I stood by her side as the procedure took place. After everything was said and done, and we had faced that hardship, she saw me head off to Vancouver, which effectively ended our relationship. I am not proud of this event and often wonder what could have been if she had decided to keep the baby.

28

WINNING A SPOT

Linda suggested other strategies to put me in top shape for the event, such as drinking lots of water. Anything that she suggested, I did. I wanted to do my best when I stood in front of the elite agents, and I was honored to represent the modelling agency I was a part of. Although I was coming from a smaller city, I wanted to be at my best.

As well as runway, we were required to create a short, thirty-second commercial. If memory serves me correctly, I wrote a deodorant commercial. I was more comfortable with runway, but I tried my best to prepare for that element of the convention.

A few weeks before Vancouver, Linda called to let me know that the photos were ready and that I should come have a look. She had booked a well-known photographer to do a photoshoot for my portfolio for Vancouver. I was excited to see the shots that the photographer took, but I was also nervous. I knew that if the photos were not right, I would be in trouble.

When I arrived at the agency, Linda was sitting at her desk looking at the pictures. She greeted me with a smile, which let me know that she was pleased with the outcome of the shoot. We both went through the images and picked out shots that she suggested should be blown up to 8"x11". She gave me a nice black portfolio binder with the name of her modelling agency in red on the front to hold the photos. I remember feeling honored.

The Faces West modelling convention is always in November and this year it was from November 10th to the 13th. November 10th was getting close, and I was as ready as I would ever be. Linda had done her job preparing me and sharing her knowledge. My checklist was complete. I had my photos blown up and in the portfolio. I had my bags packed and put aside three days early. Everything from the prep list was inside. I showed a few friends the photos from the shoot and they were impressed at how I looked. I had great support from my friends and my family. I like to think that Linda was proud of me and excited to see where I could go with modelling.

I had planned to fly to Vancouver, and was about to purchase my ticket when one of the other models going to the event — the guy who had taken first place in my first amateur fashion gala — told me that he was driving to Vancouver instead of flying to save money and invited me to ride with him. I don't think it really set in that I was going to Vancouver until he showed up at my house on the morning of November 9th, 2000 at 5:00 a.m. I placed my bags in the back hatch area of his car. I placed my portfolio carefully on the top of my luggage, making sure it wouldn't get bumped or scuffed up during the trip. We fueled up and away we went onto the open road to Vancouver.

Along the way, we conversed excitedly about what each of us thought we would see and experience when we arrived. There were times when I stared out the window, and my imagination went crazy over the idea of getting picked as an international model or possibly getting picked up by a more renowned modelling agency in a bigger city. I put no limitations on what the outcome could be. I had the mindset that even if I wasn't picked, the fact that Linda believed in me was good enough. I had already come further in modelling than I could ever have imagined. Now we would see how much further I could go.

As we drove through the flats of the Saskatchewan highway, we came to the sign for Alberta; my excitement grew at this sign that we were getting closer to Vancouver. We listened to CDs along the way. We played a lot of rock — we were both fans of AC/DC. As we travelled further into Alberta, we came to the mountains, a sign that we were almost halfway to Vancouver. Being from Saskatchewan, I always have had a great appreciation of the mountains. There was something so majestic about them, and I rarely had the opportunity to see them. Perhaps, in some strange way, I looked at their sheer size and magnitude and related them to what was in me when I thought of achieving my dreams of excelling in my modelling career.

When travelling through the mountains, my mind raced, and my friend and I shared more thoughts about the opportunities that could come from this trip. As we moved through the winding and steep roads of the mountains, I found that I couldn't stop reflecting on my journey to reach this point. All I knew was that this modelling convention was going to be a game-changer.

Before I knew it, we were in British Columbia. Amber and her husband lived in Coquitlam. I gave her a quick call to let her know that we would arrive in a few hours. We had planned to stay the night at her place. The next morning, we would get up early and drive down to the modelling convention in time for registration. We were in the home stretch of this long drive.

We entered greater Vancouver around 8:30 p.m. and arrived at my sister's house a little after 9:00 p.m. When we pulled up in front of her house, we both took a deep breath of relief. It had been a long road trip. I got out of the vehicle and had a good stretch before I opened the hatch, grabbed my bags and portfolio, and headed toward the house. I approached the door and knocked loudly. My sister answered and hugged me. I introduced my friend and we got settled.

It was late, and we had to get ready for bed as soon as possible so we could wake up feeling fresh. I put on my mask and got my spoons ready in the freezer and brushed my teeth. After I rinsed the mask off my face, I was definitely ready to sleep. I knew I would only get about seven hours of sleep, even if I fell asleep right away.

While I was trying to sleep, I couldn't help but rehearse my turns and footwork for the runway in my head. I was thinking of my smiles and little tricks like how to manipulate the structure of my jawline to look good, or how I could lightly bite on the inside of both cheeks so it would add a more chiseled look to my already high cheekbones. These were some of the things that raced through my head on the eve of the event that would ultimately change my life.

My alarm went off at 6:30 a.m. the next morning. I wasted no time. I made a light breakfast of eggs, taking care not to bloat myself with carbs. When I finished breakfast, I hopped into the shower and got ready. I did all the same things anyone might do in the morning, brushing my teeth, styling my hair, applying deodorant, and making sure I smelled great with a dash of cologne. The cold spoons trick was the only unique thing. When we were both ready, my friend and I packed up our bags again and loaded them back into the car.

When I returned to the house to thank my sister for allowing us to stay the night, she wished me the best of luck and told me that she thought I was going to do well. I gave her a hug, went back to the car. When I got into the vehicle, my friend asked if I was ready. My response was, "As ready as ever! Let's do this!" As we pulled away from the house, I knew that I felt one hundred percent confident in all my preparation.

The drive to the hotel where the modelling convention was held was quiet. I like to think it was because we were both mentally preparing ourselves for what was to come. When we arrived at the hotel, we were warmly welcomed by the bellman who directed us to the front desk to get registered. It didn't take a long time to get our keys, even though the hotel reception desk was busy and more models were showing up. I definitely felt the electric energy of the environment as more models poured into the lobby with their bags. I gave Linda a quick call to let her know I had arrived and she came down to the lobby to greet me.

When I got to my room, I hung up clothes that needed hanging and laid out the outfits that I had prepared, keeping to my space. I was sharing the room with three other male models from Linda's agency.

Then I left the room and headed to the event hall. When I arrived, I was given a number tag, and Linda told me that I had to wear it at all times. I had to wear the number even when I wasn't in the hall or participating in the convention's events because there was a chance that I could encounter agents while eating or walking around and if I didn't have my number on, I could potentially lose an opportunity.

We were told to be early for everything; it was vital that we not feel rushed. Avoiding the need to have to run around frantically was something that sounded good to me, so I made an extra effort to be early for everything and to know the times and places I was needed. I wasn't taking any unnecessary risks, whatsoever.

There was a lot of free time on the first day as most of the main events and categories I was involved in were on the second day. The free time on the first day allowed me to practice my runway turns a bit more and rehearse my commercial lines. Apparently, I was not the only one who had this idea. Many other models had the same thought. I found a long hallway that wasn't busy and was nice and quiet. I practiced all my turns over and over until I felt my nerves relaxed and I felt confident in my turns. After practicing the footwork, I went to my room and read over my lines. I did have problems getting my lines right, but as long as I didn't rush, my timing was perfect.

When I completed my preparation, I left my room and went to check out what was going on with the other models. What was everyone else up too? I went to the hall area, and many people were running around with lost looks on their faces. You could feel the pressure hanging in the air! As much as I would like to say I wasn't feeling the same pressure, I just can't. There were over six hundred models at the convention, and we were all after the same thing, a contract. You can prepare yourself as much as possible and be confident in yourself, but no matter what, it is normal to feel fear, doubt, anxiety, excitement, joy, and happiness all mixed together. I was feeling all of these emotions and I hadn't even shown my portfolio or stepped foot on the runway yet.

I walked around and mingled, meeting new people. I was getting loose, shaking my nerves. The first person I met was a girl named Selena. She was from Edmonton, Alberta. She was gorgeous. She had long brown hair, deep brown eyes, lighter brown skin. She was a bit short, but who am I to judge? She had the looks and the smile to be at this event.

Selena and I hung out for the rest of the evening. As we walked around the hotel, we told each other some stories. We talked about what modelling meant to each of us and what had brought each of us to this point. It was interesting to meet a person who had common interests in the industry. We explored the hotel a bit more and enjoyed laughs along the way. Eventually, we ended up in my hotel room, where some of the other models from Saskatoon were hanging out. We all hung out a bit more before I pulled the plug and let everyone know that tomorrow was a big day and that I would appreciate it if everyone went to another room if they wanted to continue their night. I needed to get to sleep. The next day was going to be a full day of events, and I wanted to get the best rest possible.

In the morning, I was up by 6:00 a.m. I started my day with a set of push-ups and sit-ups to get the blood flowing, followed up with light stretching. I didn't have a freezer so I couldn't freeze my spoons, but I applied a mask and later rinsed it off in the shower. I dressed in my dressiest outfit, did my hair, and gave myself a once over in the mirror to make sure I looked good. When I was ready, I headed out with my portfolio in hand and my backpack containing my robe and underwear for the runway portion.

I went to the area with the agents first thing and joined a line-up where I had to walk by each agent and show them my portfolio. Safe to say, I was quite nervous, but also very excited. I thought things like, "Just remember to smile and be yourself." I did not know what they were looking for, but I felt that if I was my happy-go-lucky self, things would be fine. Maybe a glimpse of my cheerful and positive attitude would leave the agents with a good impression of me. As I walked through the long line of agents, I found it interesting to look at the expressions on their faces. I assessed their interest or disinterest in me. Some asked questions, and others didn't. I also found it exciting when I was asked a question or complimented on a particular photo. It gave me the confidence to know that I had captured some of the agent's interest and that I may have been a fit for their agency.

For the duration of this modelling conference, it was common to see models become discouraged and upset when their numbers did not show up on the board. The board notifies the models if they have been called back to an interested agency. On the last day, I noticed many models crying, and they were clearly upset that they were not picked. I could totally understand this emotion, as they had worked hard to prepare. My number did not appear until the second to last posting on the board. I was thrilled. My name was next to an interested well-known agency that was based out of Vancouver and Toronto, Hands On Modelling (HOI). The buzz from various models who were picked was deeply contrasted with others who were crying and clearly upset. Those who were chosen were congratulating one another on their success.

On my last day, after the review and selection process of the conference, I went up to my room to change and pack my bags. I talked to my friend who had given me a ride and found out that he also made the cut, but with a major film company. We congratulated each other and said we would meet up in the lobby and head out for the long drive back to Saskatoon.

29

A MODEL'S LIFE

I was faced with a decision. Stay in Saskatoon and continue working with my current agency or to strive toward a larger dream. It wasn't a hard decision for me. I don't even think I unpacked my bag. I just packed a second one and within a week, I was on a plane back to Vancouver.

Before I left, I spent time saying goodbye to my friends. Some said that I was making a crazy decision. Some told me that modelling was a dangerous and harsh world. But I knew I was up for the challenge, so away I went.

After I arrived in Vancouver, I settled in at my sister's and set up a meeting with the agency that had taken an interest in me from the convention. The meeting went well, and I signed a one-year contract with the agency. In the months that followed, I was sent to auditions and updated my portfolio. I worked with various photographers, and I really enjoyed the faster pace of the "go, go, go" attitude it took to get my face out there. I participated in a photoshoot and fashion show for a company that was based out of New York. It was the hustle that I enjoyed the most. It was a lot of fun to meet people in the modelling world in Vancouver.

Perhaps because of the physical shape I was in, I was popular with underwear companies. I have always been shy about my body, and it wasn't easy for me to do underwear shoots and events. I knew it was all part of building a resume in the job that I was most interested in though, so it was worth it. I found a gym in Vancouver which reminded me of my home gym in Saskatoon and worked out five days per week, Monday through Friday. I later moved downtown towards the oceanfront, and moved to another gym nearby, one where the most influential bodybuilders came to work out, including famous actors who are well known for their body building physique. The gym was viewed as one of the best clubs in the greater Vancouver area, but working out in a pristine gym which had state of the art equipment didn't really do anything for me as a lifter. It didn't really didn't matter to me; I knew how to get into my zone and work toward what I needed to accomplish in whichever gym I was in.

Unfortunately, five months after I moved to Vancouver, my agency closed their office in Vancouver, choosing to focus their efforts in Toronto. I was invited to join the team in Toronto, but I declined the offer as I felt Vancouver was a great fit for me. I didn't chase another agency. I took a job working for a shoe company and put modelling on hold. I worked at the shoe store for two years. Along the way, I fell back into modelling when one day, a fashion designer walked into the shoe store, promoting his fashion show.

30

TELLING JOHN

In 2000, I was invited to my cousin Rebecca's wedding in Calgary. I decided to attend, flying first to Saskatoon for a short visit before flying back west to Calgary. When I reached Saskatoon, I met with my cousin, Mike, who was in town visiting.

Mike was really into the Bible and spoke about how great Jesus was. We had always been close and he was a guy I could trust to talk to. We were visiting downstairs in my old bedroom, in my parent's house, when I said to Mike, "I have to tell you something, but you can't tell anyone."

I asked if he would promise, and he said he would, so I told him — that John had sexually abused me as a child. I thought I would be judged and Mike would be disgusted with me, but it had quite the opposite effect. Mike became very angry and told me that I had to tell John right away that I knew that he had sexually abused me as a child. If I didn't, Mike said, he was going to "smash John's face in!" I am not sure those were his exact words, but he was extremely pissed by this news.

Although I always knew deep down that what John had done was wrong, I just didn't understand what I should do about it and if

I was to confront John, how I would do so. Mike was insistent that I tell John. He said that it would be okay and that I was safe. If John tried anything at all, Mike said he would "take him out." Even with Mike's support, I was wary of confronting John, but I also knew I could not carry the burden of this pain with me any longer. I had to make a choice and a very difficult one at that.

Mike mentioned to me that John would be at Rebecca's wedding in Calgary and that would be the time to take action.

At some point at the wedding reception, Mike came up to me and asked if I had said anything to John yet. I replied, "Not yet."

So, Mike took it upon himself to set it up. He went up to John and said, "Hey John, your cousin Niall has something he would like to talk to you about."

Now, let me rewind this a bit and let you know what I was doing at the wedding. I never, in a million years, would drink in front of my parents, let alone at an event that I was attending with them. It was an open bar, and I started with a bit of white wine. That soon changed to rye and coke, and I remember my mom looking at me and frowning at the fact that I was drinking, but I had bigger problems than her disapproval. I started to feel the booze, and I didn't want to embarrass my mom. How was I going to do this? How was I going to face my cousin, a guy who was my friend and shot pool with me? A guy who I had lived with and who had cared for me? Who was family? How would I muster up the courage to face my deepest fear? I walked up to the bartender and asked for six shots of scotch. I remember him asking me if I was serious, and I let him know I was quite serious and to pour the shots. It was about this time Mike told John that I needed to have a chat with him regarding something.

John was standing out in the parking lot at the back of the main hall, smoking a cigarette. When I walked past Mike at the back door, he patted me on the shoulder and said, "Be strong". The moment I had dreaded for years and years, I now had come face to face with.

John looked over to me and said, "Well, speak up, what did you need to talk to me about?"

I simply said ... "John, why did you do that to me when I was a kid?"

"Do what?" he replied.

"You know what I am talking about. Why did you do that to me?" He played innocent and dumb to the fact that I had remembered. He said to me that he didn't remember doing anything, and we exchanged words back and forth and then finally he said it, "I was going through puberty and experimenting." This was his excuse for his actions.

A simple excuse cannot fix a situation this traumatic. My mom always taught us to forgive, and at this time, it was precisely that thought which came to my mind. I was to forgive. I looked right at John, looked at him square in the eye and said, "I forgive you, John." And then I walked back inside.

I forgive you. It felt great to say at the time, but had I really forgiven him? At that moment, I did, yes. I forgave John to let go of the guilt and hatred. I didn't want to carry that pain anymore, so I let it go. I left it all on the battlefield.

In the weeks that followed, I told my mom what John had done to me as a child. My mother's response was as simple as it had been years ago. "Keep quiet and don't say anything more on the matter, as it would do much more harm than good if any other family members were to find out."

So, that was that. As much as I wanted to tell people, it was my mom who really put a stop to it all, and I left it at that. Only a few of the family knew about this. No one outside of the family did. It was not my intention to pinpoint my abuser, but to allow for the healing I needed and craved. What John did caused severe damage to me growing up. To those who have had something similar happen to them, I know the pain and the effects that will forever be in your thoughts. That's just the reality of it. We live, scarred for life.

In my case, when the traumatic vision of being molested came back to me, I was destroyed by the thought. I was instantly lost and confused and angry and sad and dirty. I was devastated by the knowledge that I had been taken advantage of and acted as I did. At that young age, I didn't know that what John had done was sexual abuse. At the age of seventeen, when I came to recall the abuse that had happened to me, something snapped inside me. I went from innocent thoughts to complete chaos.

31

FASHION AND DRUG LIFE

Back in Vancouver, after signing on with HOI, I kept up with my routine of working out and living a healthy lifestyle. One day, while working at the show store, a flamboyant fashion designer, named Noah, walked in and asked how many employees we had on staff. I mentioned to him there were eleven and he dropped a dozen postcards advertising a fashion show he was promoting. As I read over the promotional card, I saw that he was the designer and I ran after him. When I caught up to him, I calmly mentioned to him that I had moved to Vancouver for the very purpose of being in the fashion industry and offered my skills in fashion choreography. Noah mentioned that he was doing a shoot at his photographer's place and wrote down the address. "Come by after work," he mentioned. "We will shoot you in my clothes and see how you do."

The next thing I knew, I was offered a job as a fashion coordinator/ runway model. This job was one of the greatest, if not the greatest job I have ever had. Noah was a designer from Milan and I was excited to help him take his fashion portfolio to new heights. To do this, I needed to devise efficient fashion design plans and foster new fashion concepts. I didn't have time to read books about fashion or go to school to learn about it. I was thrown right in and was forced to learn on the fly. Whatever Noah asked of me, I was on it. For example, I coordinated advertising as well as marketing activities. This included everything from printing flyers for promotional purposes and figuring out how to get promotional material out to maximizing the potential of fashion gurus by getting them excited about the show that we were putting together.

I didn't need to attend runway or fashion shows to acquire new fashion ideas because Noah's vision in fashion was totally different from the current offerings. Our goal was to stand out and be different. We did not want to be like every other show out there. I didn't need to visit major manufacturers or merchandise markets to get new information on the latest fashion trends because we were the latest fashion trend in the making. It was my job to organize photoshoots, magazine events, and fashion shows. When it came time to select garments and accessories that were used for shows, we would hit the streets and ask people if they were interested in showcasing their jewelry or perhaps a particular brand of sunglasses or shoes. Noah made me business cards; one printed with the title Assistant Fashion Director, and the other Model Scout.

Searching for the talent was one of the tasks that I was responsible for. I had to make sure that they could represent Noah's brand in the manner that he wanted. I gave my business cards to potential male and female models. For every fifty, "No's," there was one, "Yes." All I could do was to talk to more people and show their faces to Noah. We needed over twenty models for each show, so I had to hustle all the time, giving my best effort. We typically ended up with a ratio of 70/30, women to men. I was a huge factor in making Noah's vision come to life. It was a great experience, and I gained skills in this job that will be with me forever.

Working with Noah, I partied hard as we travelled from city to city; places like Vancouver, Calgary, Edmonton, Ottawa, and Toronto. I met a lot of people who loved drugs and loved to party. Suddenly, I was once again on a path of destruction, finding myself always pushing the limits because I thought I had no limits when it came to the consumption of drugs. I would try anything once, and if I liked it, I would do more.

On one fashion tour in 2002, I was at a club in Calgary. There was no shortage of drugs and alcohol. I started the night by mixing MDMA (Ecstasy) and hard booze with the occasional line of cocaine. MDMA makes you feel warm and fuzzy and gives you a desire to connect and be touched, and often leads to sex.

I asked the attractive girl who was sitting next to me with her guy friend if she cared for a rail of cocaine. She said she would love one. I invited her guy friend to have one too. When he went to the bathroom, she started making out with me, and when he returned, she continued to talk to him while rubbing my leg under the table. Later that night, she ditched her guy friend, and, well, I will leave the rest to your imagination as to what happened next. Cocaine was influential in many ways.

On other trips to Calgary, we would go to a club that had individual booths with see-through drapes surrounding them. I would make my rounds, saying my hellos, and I would find some product. I would chat it up with some girls, and we would do some lines and have some drinks. Before I knew it, the girls would be taking off their tops, and I would be doing rails off their breasts and other body parts. Then we would round up the crew and see where the night took us.

It was a fast life filled with beautiful women and surrounded by people who knew all the right people to make the night even better. It seemed that I always knew someone who had a connection to people who had friends in high places; people with a lot of money and who were tremendously connected in the fashion industry.

It was a fast life with only one possible outcome.

32

MEETING KAT AND KETAMINE

Vancouver was where I first really experienced the effect of mixing drugs. MDMA was a lot different than cocaine. This stuff would make me absolutely crazy. On "Molly," my vision would be messed up. Sometimes while I was in a club, I wouldn't be able to tell if I was even walking straight. One time, I walked slanted all night. My eyes couldn't focus. The whole bar was strobe lights. The heavy bass from the speakers shook my insides. I couldn't see straight and kept bumping into people, even though I would try to avoid them. I tried to get to the third floor to the VIP room where the rest of the group was partying. I needed to find the elevator that would take me up there, but I had real trouble finding it. I eventually straightened out enough as the drug wore off enough that I could realize what was happening around me. I grabbed a drink and chilled out a bit before heading up to the VIP room. I knew once I went up there, I would quickly get out of control again and end up doing rails of cocaine to get numb. I knew I did not have control of my body, and at the same time, I knew I loved it.

Another time in 2002, I was on Granville Street in downtown Vancouver. I was at a small after-hours club, and I was ripped on ecstasy. I arrived with a couple of friends, but they ended up leaving, but I wasn't ready to stop partying. I was a mess. So high. But I was able to focus enough to notice a super-hot woman across the dance floor. My eyes kept going back to her. She was wearing a tight white tank top and cargo style army pants. She had an athletic build and nicely toned arms. The music was blasting, and she was dancing like crazy; she looked super sexy while she danced. I went up to her and told her that I thought she looked hot and that she was incredibly sexy. She came closer to me and said that she thought I was sexy myself. She grabbed my hands and pulled me to her body and started dancing with me. Eventually, she rubbed up against me and wrapped me up with her arms.

We danced for a while until there was commotion and everyone had started dispersing in different directions. I was so high I didn't even notice that the lights had been turned on and the music had stopped. I had lost sight of the girl I was dancing with, and I was standing there in a daze with no clue of what was going on. People were walking and running in all different directions. I heard someone say in my direction that the police had shown up and to exit the building. I was still standing there when I felt a hand grab my arm, and someone say, "Come with me." It was the girl I had been dancing with, Kat.

She grabbed my arm and told me to look straight and walk normally. What was normal? I was a mess. How does one act or look normal when your brain is mush, and you are incredibly high on drugs?

I can remember her guiding me toward the front doors. It was just starting to get light out, and there were a lot of people in the streets. There were roughly seven to eight of us and we all started walking in a group. After we had walked a long way, she mentioned that these people were friends of hers and that it was all good. We had a place to go to and that I didn't need to worry.

As we walked, we were doing little bumps of ketamine and cocaine. A bump is a small amount of coke placed on your hand that you then suck up your nose. Ketamine was new to me, and I had not done it before that night. It was a totally different high. Perhaps because it was a horse tranquilizer, who knows, but if you were not careful, you could go into what's called the "K" hole. I wanted to take lines of this stuff, but she was very familiar with it and made sure I didn't take too many bumps. She had this neat little scoop that would give you the perfect sized small bump and then another little bumper filled with cocaine. A bumper is a small contraption that you can load by turning a dial. It measures out a small amount and you sniff the bump of cocaine. K is a downer and coke is an upper — you switch back and forth when one high is stronger than the other. She turned a dial and tipped it over which loaded the bumper and then set the dial again and put the bumper up to my nose, and I sucked up the product through my nose. Every time she would offer me a bump, I said yes.

We ended up at some guy's house that Kat knew. I was obviously there with Kat and attracted to her, but you would be surprised what drugs can do to your mind and in what direction it may choose to go. A guy in the group made it clear that he thought I was attractive. Everyone was doing drugs and making out a bit. I remember another guy asking me if he could take a picture of me with my shirt off. He was a little pushy about it and that made me feel uncomfortable.

Eventually, Kat said that she needed to go home. As we got ready to leave and part ways, I asked her what her plans were for the rest of her day. She replied, "I have to go to work tonight." I was in shock. I asked her quickly what she did for work. "I am a nurse," she said.

She walked back toward me, took a pen out of her bag, wrote her name and number on a piece of paper. She took out the bumper she had, offered me one last bump, gave me a kiss — and left. She went her way, and I started my journey home. I remember trying to look normal as I walked in the bright daylight. I felt like people were looking at me strangely. I knew I didn't look as good as I did when I got ready the night before; I definitely knew that.

33

DOWNSIDE OF K

A few weeks later, Kat and I met up again, but this time it was for dinner and drinks at her place. When I got there, she was just getting out of the shower. She met me at the door in her robe and then returned to her room to get ready while I waited. She said I could have a seat on the sofa and that she would be right out. When she came out, she kissed me and proceeded to the kitchen. She reached up above the fridge and brought down a glass baking pan. The bottom of the pan was covered with a white powdered substance an inch deep. She walked into the living room and placed a pile of the substance on coffee table in front of me. She did a line and I did a line. We sat and talked for a bit, and then it hit me, I was wrecked.

Everything went into slow motion. I couldn't control myself. Even though I tried to focus, there was just no way. I attempted to carry on a normal conversation. She was handling the drug much better than I was. Obviously, she did ketamine often and this was only my second time trying it. Soon I couldn't talk properly, but I knew it was funny, and we both started to laugh really hard. I asked for another line, and she laughed again, thinking it was funny that I was so high and yet was still asking her for another line. We did another line.

When I had arrived, Kat hadn't finished drying her hair, so she went back to the bedroom to finish getting ready. While she was in the room, she yelled out to me, asking if I would be able to take the chicken out of the oven because it was ready.

I said, "Yeah no problem," and got up off of the couch and walked into the kitchen. I proceeded to the oven and opened the door. I was hit by a blast of heat that seemed to burn my face and arms as if a huge flame jumped out at me and burnt me. I jumped back from the oven, standing about two feet back from it. I grabbed the oven mitts and slowly approached the open oven door. I am not sure what the problem was, but the heat was so intense that I couldn't get close to touching the pan that the chicken was in. I continued to try to get close enough to the pan to pick it up, but every time I would get close, the heat was overwhelming; it was as if I was putting my hands directly into a blazing fire. I couldn't get close enough even to pick the pan up.

Kat came into the kitchen and saw me creeping up to the oven with my face turned away. She asked, "What are you doing?"

I was still not able to speak correctly because of the effects of the drugs and stuttered, "I am trying to take the chicken out, but I can't because of the heat."

She laughed and asked for the oven mitts. She reached in the oven and grabbed the chicken with no problem. I was amazed and asked her how she was able to withstand the extreme heat. She mentioned that it wasn't even hot and continued to laugh. We finished prepping the food together and finally ate. Later that night we watched a movie and continued to do bumps. Mine were smaller than hers, as it was apparent that the drug had more of an effect on me than it did on her. I could not handle it as she could. I was amazed that she had a whole pan full of this stuff; that was crazy. But what was crazier than her drug tolerance was the fact that she sourced the drug from the hospital where she worked. She was a nurse and could get it at will.

That was my first real experience with using the drug ketamine. It is a pretty powerful drug. Just like any other drug or substance, if you don't respect it, it can bring you a world of hurt. By world of hurt, I am talking about the "K" hole. An appropriate comparison would be for you to imagine being thrown into a very deep pit where you are surrounded by blackness. You can't move. Your conscious state of mind is blacked out, your eyes are closed, and when you try to open them, you cannot focus. You can hear things, and you are aware slightly of what is happening around you, but you cannot move or function well. It is a place you never want to be.

34

HIGH AND SUCCESSFUL

The drugs continued to flow, but so did my modelling career. Despite my partying, I was able to reach new heights and become successful within the fashion industry. Noah and I were leaders in Vancouver's fashion scene. We were able to feed off one another's ideas, and it wasn't long before we put the wheels in motion for a magnificent spectacle — a Fashion Gala like no other.

As we implemented our crazy concepts, a bigger picture formed. The idea was to remove typical stereotypes of fashion shows by incorporating hip hop dancers on the stage at the same time as the models. It was my job to come up with the choreography and to coordinate the right timing of the music to allow the models to walk to the beat while the dancers showcased their talents.

First, we needed models. We held auditions, or cold calls as the industry refers to them. This is where a model shows up at the office, and we conduct a short interview. I contacted many modelling agencies and let agents know what we were planning on doing so they could send who they thought would be a great fit for the fashion gala. We needed to align the number of models with the number of outfits and calculate how many changes each model needed. The girls had three wardrobe changes while the guys only had two. This was normal as the women's line was usually larger than the men's.

Next, it was time to find the location, staging, and lighting for the show. These tasks were generally easy, but they had some challenges. We needed to make sure that the audio and lighting were capable of achieving what we envisioned. We wanted various graphics displayed on large screens on the side and background of the stage throughout the show.

After we found the right setup for our vision, it was easy to start to create buzz for the show. We held our first show in Vancouver. We sold out quickly and premiered to a packed house. For our second event, we had a much larger venue and a more bigger audience with more high-profile people attending.

Then we had a bigger idea. Motorcycles.

We found the perfect entrance music — the sound of a Formula 1 race car revving at various RPMs with a catchy beat in the background. I called a local motorcycle shop and asked for sponsorship, which allowed us to use various styles of motorcycles for the Fashion Gala. The motorcycle shop gave us six bikes and several stylish motorcycle jackets to showcase. We agreed that the bikes, along with the gear and sponsor banner, were to be delivered on the day of the event.

The most difficult part of the show was preparing the press release and contacting the people to invite. I wrote many emails, making them personal to each VIP. Some invites were for magazines, some were for television stations, and some were for writers who represented news companies. To market the event, we printed 2,500 poster flyers and then went out and handed them to individuals and businesses throughout downtown Vancouver.

It was exciting sometimes to hear, "Hey, are you those guys who put that fashion show with the hip hop dancers?"

"Yes, that was us," I would reply.

"That show was amazing!" they would say.

"Well thank you, hope to see you at the next one!" I would reply.

To plan the show, I stayed up countless days, drinking coffee, and working myself to exhaustion. I went out night after night to create a buzz about the next grand gala we were staging. When we reached what I call the safe point — the time when there isn't much left to accomplish in planning — the pace and pressure still didn't stop. I listened to our chosen music to coordinate the footwork and steps of the models. I drew a T-shaped stage and arrows in the directions the models had to walk, where they had to stop, and where they closed in on one another's paths. The planning of the choreography was where I was able to really utilize the fashion event skills I had learned back home in Saskatoon.

At this point in planning, we had videographers, photographers, staging, lighting, press releases, media, models, hairdressers, makeup artists, dancers, music, marketing, clothing, the venue, and sponsors. We even arranged for a liquor license for the gala.

We didn't have a lot of time to rehearse for the show, so I went to the mall and taped a 'T' on the ground and rehearsed individually with the models. Some models were well trained in their footwork, others were not. I showed them what turns they needed to use in the show and sent them home to practice, emphasizing the importance of practicing. They were a part of a real shift in the fashion world; we were breaking barriers, and each of us played a significant role in doing it as a team.

The work still didn't stop there. We needed to work on the selection and coordination of the outfits. I wanted to make sure Noah was happy with what I had put together and that it complemented his vision. This took some time, but eventually everything fell into place and the planning was complete.

After the planning ended, but before the final rehearsals began, the staging, lighting, and backdrop needed to be set up. A platform that we could safely ride a motorcycle on as we drove the machines up on stage needed to be designed; the grade of the ramp had to be at an angle that allowed the bikes to pass without hitting the bottom of the fairing. (Fairing is an external metal or plastic structure added to increase streamlining and reduce drag, especially on a high-performance car or motorcycle.)

Once the staging was set up, we had a night of rehearsals. This was where things got complicated, as it was tough to get everyone on the same page. When I was confident that no one would forget what we had reviewed, the models were allowed to go home and get the rest that was needed to be full of life for the gala.

On the day of the event, I didn't feel a lot of pressure. Everyone was in high spirits, and I felt confident that we would have a successful fashion gala. We were so calm that before the event, a few of us who knew how to ride sport bikes went on a little tear through the city. We did not wear helmets or anything of the sort. It was kind of a quick rush before people started to show up. We had one last rehearsal and soon it was showtime. I have to say that this gala came together well. I was very proud.

The bikes rolled into the building quietly, engines turned off. As the crowd sat and anticipated the beginning of the fashion show, the lights turned off, and the only lights that could be seen were the spotlights placed strategically around the room. Smoke from dry ice machines filled the room. Then the music started, and the sound of the Ferrari Indy cars were heard. The bikes were fired up, and the double doors swung open. This allowed the bright light into the room, and we drove the bikes through a path that we had blocked off from the crowd. It was an amazing start to a fashion show. I and one other model drove our bikes up on the stage. After the entrance, I parked next to the stage and ran to the back area to get ready to model my first outfit. As I was the head model for the fashion show and the brand, I was the starting model to open the gala.

One by one, the models came out, and it was beautiful to watch. The dancers were smiling and having fun, and the models on stage entertained the crowd. It was symmetry in motion. As the last model walked off the stage, we all hit the stage one more time, showcasing the last outfits. We stayed on the stage while the designer took the stage, walking hand in hand with one of our models. We had an amazing team and, even today, I am thankful that I could execute a fantastic show with such an extraordinary group of people.

But as our success rose, so did the pressure. Noah would need me to be available almost 24/7. I used drugs to help me stay awake and make deadlines. Noah knew the drugs were helping me to stay awake and complete the tasks at hand and he kept enough drugs on hand to ensure I was meeting his goals. As our popularity started to really grow, we were the hype of fashion in Vancouver. Every Fashion

Gala we put on sold out and we started searching for bigger venues and took our show on the road.

The drugs really started flowing. People think, "It will never happen to me," but the pressure to fit in is huge. And fitting in means drug use and partying hard. I remember going to parties in Calgary with a group of friends in the fashion industry. We would hit the clubs in a limo, entering clubs with our VIP status. We would stop, pick up some women, and do rails of cocaine off their bodies in the back of the limo. It was a crazy time. When the nightclubs would close, we would head to a condo party and bring and invite as many people as we possibly could. At one party, a guy dropped on the table a wrapped brick of blow worth about $30,000. He ripped the top open, took a scoop, and dropped a quarter of blow in front of everyone at the table. He made sure everyone at the party was taken care of, going from room to room asking if anyone needed coke. These parties were crazy; naked girls in one room doing body bumps off each other, and people having sex right out in the open while people were sitting and talking right beside them.

At that particular party everyone was ripped on cocaine and drank until 9:00 a.m. I left the house with a buddy who had rested long enough to drive. In the car, he told me that he thought I was pretty hardcore for not sleeping all night and just continuing to party. I was, for the most part, always the last man standing. Not many people could outlast me, and this continued for years to come.

We would usually leave a party in the morning, rest quickly, and then get ready for the next big night. It was a crazy system of party after party while meeting many new people along the way who all enjoyed the same lifestyle. No matter which club we went to, I rarely ever had to wait in line, regardless of the city I was in. For the most part, I always knew a core group of friends that could get me into any club, at any time. I always made sure I introduced myself to the owners, and I always knew that most of them were into cocaine. If they weren't, they knew who had it and who was selling it in their establishment. I would often get free booze and end up at their afterhours party, doing cocaine through the night and into the early morning hours. I took their business cards and was sure to send them a thank you for their hospitality — usually designer belt buckles or other product.

I liked to think I was in control of the drugs, but as I look back on it now, the drugs had a firm hold on me.

35

FLIRTING WITH HEROIN

Cocaine was the food I was feeding my demons. The devil himself was running my life. The grasp and the squeeze I felt on my soul was unbearable.

I was looking for a new high, something next level. This is when I was formally introduced to heroin by my friend from the shoe store. I had never tried heroin before and he warned me that the drug was potent and extreme. I told him I was up for trying it at least once.

We met a car in a parking lot to pick up the drug. We didn't waste any time, and once the exchange in money for product was complete, I asked if they would prepare the drug so I could try it immediately. Before I took my first hit, I was warned that I would likely throw up. I sloughed off the warning, reminding them that I was quite experienced. I had no worries that I could handle it.

I was wrong. As soon as I exhaled, the effect hit so fast and so hard that I couldn't help but throw up. The front passenger hopped out and opened the door to let me out. I did what I had to do and then settled back down in the rear seat and found my center as the drug took full effect. It was an intense high, a high that I was never able to reach before, and I liked it. A lot. I liked it so much that I decided then and there I was choosing this drug over my previous favorite choice of cocaine.

The drug gave me that next level high I was craving. But after a few weeks, I realized that if I kept on this path, I was sure I would start needing to take it in the vein, the next step in getting a higher high. I wasn't prepared to try that, so I quit — and thank goodness I did.

I returned to cocaine. By now, I had now experienced all the possible drugs that I knew with the exception of peyote (which contains mescaline, a hallucinogenic drug). The harsh truth is I didn't think I wanted to make it to twenty-five.

This was my life for many years. Swallowed up in a wild lifestyle and addicted to drugs. From the age of twenty-five to the age of thirty-seven, I was a slave to drugs and addicted to cocaine.

36

CRACK IN SASKATOON

When I was working in the mall at the shoe store, I had a friend who worked in one of the other sister stores. He and I would often get together and drink whiskey and use cocaine. Whisky and cocaine always went hand in hand. When I started to drink, the need for cocaine would never be far behind — and it was always accessible. Although I thought I was in control, I was far from it.

During the Boxing Week sale at the store, I was introduced to a more potent drug that would give me a great burst of energy. This drug was speed, which is tiny crystals that are crushed up and turned into a fine powder. Now, you don't need a lot of speed to get your mind and body racing. My friend and I were on the drug for days and days. Our performance at work was greater than our other co-workers. The drug gave us an advantage; we were faster and sharper. My co-worker and I took top sales that year, and I am not talking by a few hundred dollars. We were thousands ahead of the other workers.

In addition to the shoe store, I continued to work with Noah as well as modelling with HOI. I modelled underwear and did various other smaller commercial parts and TV ads. I was involved in fashion and doing what I loved to do—runway modelling and coordinating fashion galas. I was in great shape, as I worked out five days a week. I used skin products to help keep my skin looking great and healthy.

In late 2002, with my bonus cheque from the shoe store and the money made from modelling, I decided to visit my friends and family in Saskatoon. I told my roommate that I would be back in a couple weeks. I had roughly $4,000 saved up because I wanted to be able to do whatever I wanted when I went home, whether it was going for dinner or drinks with friends, or whatever the case may be. My goal was to go back cashed up and not have to worry if I wanted to pick up a check. I grew up with hand-me-downs and clothes bought from low-cost department stores and now I was returning home wearing $800 high fashion jeans, shoes worth $200, shirts that cost $150, and a watch worth a cool $500. I was looking great and feeling great. I was living in Vancouver, chasing my dream of modelling.

Coming back to Saskatoon was a poor decision.

I was shocked when I first got back. I found many of my friends hooked on a new phase of drugs. Everyone was doing it, and I mean everyone. 90% of the people I knew were either doing it or had tried it. I was only supposed to be in Saskatoon for a visit, a maximum of ten days. I ended up staying for over four months.

My friends were "hooked on a feeling." Trey, Marcus, Damian and before long, I fell victim to this terrible drug. One night we were at my buddy Trey's apartment. Marcus was living with Trey as well. The area wasn't in the horrible area of the city, but it was bad enough. We all caught up and shared stories.

I remember sitting on the couch, when Trey pulled out a 600 ml empty pop bottle. Next came a little black kit the size of a fingernail manicure kit. Trey unzipped it and revealed the contents: a piece of steel wool (like the kind used to wash pans), various scraping tools, pins, small squares of tinfoil, and lighters. I watched as Trey ripped a small piece of steel wool off and heated it with a lighter, burning off whatever chemical or coating was on it.

Marcus then took the pop bottle and with his lighter heated a spot on the side of the bottle. The purpose was to soften the plastic enough to poke the tube of a pen through it. He took a piece of chewed up bubble gum and wrapped it around the hole where the pen was shoved into the pop bottle. The gum created a seal so the smoke wouldn't escape. The pen was a little way into the pop bottle and three-quarters of the way out. He was creating a pipe that we would be smoking the drug through once the cocaine was heated and converted from powder to rock form.

Crack is a pretty fast-acting drug. You quickly got what's called a "ringer," as in "ring your bell." After watching Marcus and Trey take a hit off the pipe, it was my turn. I can remember being excited to try a new drug and this new process. I took the pipe and exhaled all the breath I had before I started sucking in on the pen straw, inhaling the smoke. I listened to Trey and Marcus' instructions as I held it in the best I could. After a while, I exhaled and wow, what a feeling. It was good, and I was high. The effects of the drug were in full force.

This high, though, was short-lived. It left as fast as it came. After four to five minutes, I wanted another one.

The high is so short that you continually chase it and before long, my friends and I had gone through all their money and mine.

My friend Marcus worked at a bar, so sometimes people would give him tips in crack rocks, or if he had set up several deals, he would get some for being a hustler and leading people to his supplier. He was a middle man, and everyone knew where to go if they wanted crack.

What started as a few friends sitting around getting high soon turned into a steady stream of people coming and going from Marcus' house. They stopped in, got us high (because Marcus would get them hooked up), and they would share what they had and get more to take away. All day and all night, this would continue; it was a vicious cycle. Marcus had a great system; it was flawless. He could get high all the time, and he didn't want to do it by himself, so he shared with us.

I only went back to my parents' house when I knew no one would home. I would quickly shower and change my clothes and go back to Marcus's place. At first, we would only sit at the apartment and smoke it. Then, we went to other people's dives to smoke it with people we had never met before. There was always a friend of a friend that knew someone who smoked crack, and if they had the money to buy it, that is where we went. We followed the crack wherever it led and did whatever we had to do to get it.

It wasn't long before I gave my watch away. I traded the beautiful watch that cost me $500 to some crack-slinging bum for two grams, a street value of $120. Things went seriously downhill from there, as I started stealing from my parents. I would sneak into their bedroom when they were at work or out for the evening, and snoop in their closet where I knew they had cash in small bills and a jar of loose change. I would take a bit here and a bit there, nothing that I thought they would ever notice. They didn't — until the day finally came when my parents wanted to exchange their jar of coins for bills. To their surprise, most of the money was gone. I will never forget the look of hurt on my mother's face the day she came up to me and asked me if I had taken the money. I was busted red-handed with my "hand in the cookie jar," as they say.

When my mother asked me if it was me that took the money, I didn't deny it. I told her straight up, "Yes, Mom, it was me, I took your money."

"Do you know your dad and I have been saving that money for months and months for our trip we were planning. What are we to do now? We can't afford to go on our trip now."

Do you want to talk about pain in your heart? I had known I was doing terrible, terrible things, but the drugs had a tight grip on me, and my mother didn't know it. It is easy for me to blame it on the drugs, but when you're high for days and chasing the next opportunity to get high, you will do anything. Lie, cheat, steal; whatever it takes.

I remember Trey slowly weaning himself off of crack. He was the first one to realize what it was doing to all of us. It wasn't long after he quit, he looked at me and said, "Niall, can I talk to you, brother? What are you doing, man? Man, you are so much better than this. Do you not remember what you were doing? You live in Vancouver man. You need to stop this shit, go back and finish what you started. I am proud of you, man. You have done well. Better than any of us."

I gave him a brotherly hug and said, "Thanks for saying that."

It opened my eyes. Trey and I were on the road to recovery. We did flip from time to time, but our crack use was no longer an all-day, every-day event.

Our main concern was now Marcus. He wasn't slowing down; he was getting worse. He was oblivious to what was occurring around him and moved like he was half asleep. There were times when he would come home with some girl after a hard night of partying and they would pass out in his room. Trey and I would sneak into the room and clap our hands, or bang a pot and lid together, or run the vacuum — anything to see if they would wake up. If they did, we would pretend we were watching TV in the living room and give them time to fall back asleep. If they didn't wake up, game on! We would put shaving cream on Marcus' hand and tickle his nose, and he would naturally go to itch his nose and get himself with the shaving cream. Trey and I thought it was pretty funny.

One time when Marcus had passed out on the couch, Trey went to the bathroom and found some hair clippers. Trey turned the clipper on to see if the loud buzzing sound would wake Marcus, but after partying, Marcus was a heavy sleeper. Trey slowly crept closer and closer until he was finally buzzing Marcus' hair. He made a small bald spot on the back of Marcus' head, one inch by two inches. Then I took the clippers from Trey and made that bald patch into a rather large bald patch, two and a half inches by three inches. We put the clippers away and waited.

Finally, Marcus woke up, and Trey and I just sat there waiting for Marcus to notice. Still stoned, he got up off the couch and headed to the shower to get ready for work. There was no doubt in our minds that at any minute we would hear a loud scream, but to our amazement, nothing happened. If there was one thing about Marcus, it was that he loved his hair. He would sit in front of the mirror, sometimes for twenty to thirty minutes placing each strand in place. He had curly hair, so when one curl was out of place, he had a specific place for it.

Before heading out the door, he stood in the front hall in front of a huge mirror hung, playing with his hair. Trey and I were trying so hard not to laugh, as Marcus was running his fingers right over the bald spot. I thought: Man, those drugs have to be really good for him not to notice such a huge bald spot shaved in the back of his head. Marcus went to work, and apparently no one ever said anything to him about the bald spot because he still didn't know about it when he came home.

The fact of the matter was that there was just no stopping Marcus with his crack use. As time continued, Trey and I started to worry more and more. Finally, Trey and I discussed that we needed to do something to help Marcus. It was time to make a call to Abigail, Marcus' mom. We wanted to let her know that Marcus had a serious problem and that he needed help. I called Abigail and she drove into the city and picked him up. She took him to the town where she and her daughter ran a hotel. Marcus was now out of the city and away from anyone who could get him any drugs. We had successfully gotten him somewhere safe. We were all free of it and very thankful.

Marcus called Trey's phone once in a while and thanked us for what we did. Both Trey and I felt good that Marcus was doing well. A month after he left Saskatoon, the phone rang. I could hear Trey talking to Marcus, letting him know, "It wasn't me but ... well okay, maybe I did the little spot, but NialI was the one who really shaved the big bald spot on your head."

What happened was that Marcus was getting a haircut from his mom, and she asked, "Why do you have a big bald spot shaved in the back of your hair, Marcus?"

I wish I could have been there to see the look on his face! To see Marcus jump out of the chair and have a look for himself; the look of shock would have been priceless to see.

Let me tell you, when you survive hitting rock bottom on crack, you genuinely learn the dangers. I went from having success in modelling, having nice things, and living a clean, healthy lifestyle to having absolutely nothing in four months. It happens fast, and if friends who genuinely care about you do not surround you, you're done — you're a goner, game over. If Trey hadn't said something to me, and we didn't do anything for Marcus, I honestly believe I wouldn't be here writing to you.

37

RESPECTING THE GAME

I wasn't using crack anymore, but I was still using the raw form, cocaine. This drug made me feel great, like I was on top of the world. The high was so great that ultimately, it worked to destroy me and everything that surrounded me. I had always been able to hide the physical effects of drug use, but now I was beginning to look haggard and sketched out.

Over the years, I had always been an incredibly social and likable guy. I had the gift of gab and could make friends everywhere I went. It didn't matter what city or province; I could meet a varied group of people. Some were poor or grungy-dressed, others were well dressed and had great jobs, and some were just ordinary middle-class people. I was like a chameleon; I was able to adapt and speak in terms that were relatable to all types of people. So, in doing this, I surrounded myself with the people who did the drug in many different circles of friends.

In the drug world, you have to be careful and street smart. It is safe to say, I am educated when it comes to being street smart. Back home in Saskatoon, I grew to know a lot about cocaine. I knew various runners. A runner is the minion who drives all over the city and drops off bags of cocaine to people. Runners knew other dealers, and other dealers had various types of the drug. My goal was always to find the dealer who had the best quality and get the most value for the amount of money I would spend. Getting to know various dealers was high on my priority list. Like I mentioned before, the drug world is no joke. You make a wrong move, cross or betray the wrong person and you could get hurt or even disappear. I was always careful and made exact moves. I was savvy at recognizing the situation and adapting to it. Now obviously, I made some mistakes, but in the drug world, you don't often make a wrong decision two times without consequences.

I knew the runners and I knew the dealers, and soon I would come to know the bosses. "The bosses" were the guys at the top of the food chain of the local cocaine train. Knowing these guys puts you in constant danger. Things can change in an instant. The only people who are bigger and meaner than these guys were the people who would supply the bosses, the "organized crime bosses." I was a guy who could be trusted, and I never gave any reason for them not to believe me; I knew the dangers.

In Saskatoon, many of my friends were in the same circles, and we all existed, for the most part, in harmony. It was my secret society. I was accepted by many and disliked by few. Over time, I was safe. I had the muscle, and I knew I could call upon the right people if ever I needed to and that they would have my back. I grew to know so many people in the city that there was not a place I could go and not know someone. I was shaking hands and asking the people I bumped into how they were doing and was connected everywhere I went. It is like that even today. It is a neat feeling knowing so many people and being involved in so many people's lives.

38

GETTING BACK MY LIFE

Noah eventually called me with concern for what I was doing. I did not want to disclose why I was stuck in Saskatoon. But the truth was, I had lost all my money and belongings to my addictions. After telling Noah my financial situation, he offered to buy my ticket back to Vancouver so we could continue our fashion venture together. Thankfully, my roommate Jamison agreed to take me back. I returned to the apartment in Langley, my job at the shoe store, and started rebuilding my health and physique so I could again be in the public eye.

The gym I started to attend was located in a strip mall. It was there that I thought I was in good enough shape to try my first spin class. I had heard these classes were challenging, so I thought it would be a good match for my fitness plan. I told myself that what the instructor could do, I could also do, so as I began my first class, I kept pace with the instructor. Ten minutes in, I could feel that I was already getting fatigued, and I still had thirty minutes left!

I pushed myself to keep up with the instructor and soon knew that this was a horrible idea! I was burning all over, I was short of breath, and my muscles were definitely fatigued. An unpleasant feeling started to come over me; I had pushed and tried my best, but I eventually vomited right in the spin class. I could barely get off of the bike to clean up after myself.

Although my first spin class wasn't a pleasant experience, but it did teach me a lesson. No matter how great of shape I thought I was in, it takes time to get good at something new. What was I thinking? I really had thought that I could just jump in and keep pace with someone who had been doing this for some time, possibly years? I didn't quit the class, but I sure listened to my body the next time and slowed the pace when I needed to. Eventually, I was able to do well in the spin class. I truly enjoyed pacing myself according to how my body felt while knowing what my body couldn't handle.

There is nothing wrong with pushing yourself to your limits. I think it is a good thing to push your limits in all aspects of your life. In my opinion, a lot of people never get to see their full potential because they are scared of other people's opinions about what they might be able to accomplish in life. Other people's negative opinions can cripple you if you allow it. I feel you should always believe in what you think you can accomplish in life no matter what other people might say.

My friend, Joe, asked me to check out another gym. When I first entered the space, it was as if I had walked into a time machine and was sent back into the past. The gym had the exact feeling, smell, and weights of the gym that I first started at in Saskatoon — it felt like the Iron Works Gym. Even the machines were the same color. There were a lot of mirrors everywhere. This was my new gym, no question.

In 2003, I continued to meet new people, including a few women. Janelle worked in the same mall as where the shoe store was, and we started to go on dates during her lunch breaks. Our lunches were filled with great conversations and a lot of laughter. Janelle had blonde hair and a great smile. At six feet, she was taller than me, a fact that didn't bother me. Janelle came to every fashion show and I reserved a seat for her in the front row. Something was amazing about having my girlfriend beside the stage while I modelled. As much as I tried not to look at her, I couldn't help myself. I would glance over to see her, and she always had a great big smile on her face and was cheering me on from the side of the stage. When I saw her, I would smile at the end of my poses, which actually made it easier for me because my smiles were not forced, and the photographers from the roped-off area got great shots.

Janelle was never worried about or jealous of the models that I worked with. She was strong-minded. She knew that after all the glitz and glamour was over, I was coming home with her. She complimented me as a partner. For example, she knew how to work a crowd, and if we were at a high-end event, she was always smiling and mingling.

Maybe my life was getting back on track.

39

TOO GOOD TO LAST

One of our next shows was filmed live for MTV at their studio in downtown Vancouver on Robson Street. It was exciting to plan because, like most of our shows, it was the first of its kind. We always challenged the way that people thought fashion should be represented. The stereotype was skinny, anorexic-looking girls on stage that walked with no life or excitement. We were not about that at all. We put more than one model on stage at a time, models of all shapes and sizes. They interacted with the crowd, smiling and showing they were enjoying themselves. We also incorporated unique elements, such as the hip hop dancers and motorcycles. Unfortunately, we would not be able to ride motorcycles into the MTV set, so new choreography was required.

The process of putting on a live televised fashion show adds considerable pressure. Not only do we have the viewers next to the stage, but we have thousands tuning in as well. These additional viewers raises the bar really fast.

The night before the big show we had rehearsals; we had to make sure that everyone on the crew was ready to perform. After the rehearsal, we told everyone to meet at the back of the building at 10:00 a.m. sharp the next morning.

Noah and I had organized a limo and a Porsche convertible for a marketing stunt the next day. In the morning, we piled into the limo and convertible, set to get crazy in the streets on the way to the show. There were girls in the convertible with Noah and I and several models were in the limo following the Porsche. At the first break in the traffic, I jumped out of the limo and into the Porsche with Noah and the girls. At each new light, we changed spots from one vehicle to the other, playing a game of musical chairs but with cars in traffic. It was hilarious and fun! Sometimes, at a red light, we all got out of the vehicles and danced in the streets. We were loving life and embraced the happiness and excitement over our huge show.

We arrived at the studio and dropped most of the models off at the back of the building before Noah and I drove around to the front. When we pulled up to the studio, there was a large group of people waiting and cheering. The limo stopped, and it was showtime. I exited the limo first, then two girls followed, and then Noah. The film crew and the photographers fought through the crowd to get the shots they wanted. It was interesting to have people cheering for us. We had a following, and it was only our third show!

We entered the studio, and I led us back to the staging area where the models were gathered. I made sure wardrobe was ready, and the dressers were prepared and organized. The show started, and everyone did an amazing job. Everything went smoothly. Paying attention to the small details left no room for error.

After the show, we had a white glove after-party at Noah's rented house. It was a 5,000 square foot house with a backyard swimming pool, two tennis courts, and fruit trees. It was like something from a movie. Being a small-city boy from Saskatoon who grew up in a 900 square foot house, this was like living in a dream.

We invited all of our movie industry and fashion guru acquaintances. We had made friends who were working on a movie production starring several well-known actors.

Noah had put me in charge of making sure everything went well. In preparation for the party, we had bought a lot of booze, and the catering company had worked on the presentation of the plates and hors d'oeuvres. The pool had been cleaned, and the landscaper had trimmed and cleaned up the yard. The bar was set up, and everything came together wonderfully.

Guests started to show up slowly, but it quickly became busier and busier. As I was one of the hosts, I tried to stay on top of everything, but I soon let that goal go out of the window. There were about three hundred people at the house, and the party was only getting bigger. The whole house was packed! We had a hot tub in the basement, and people were piled in there. It had a max limit of twenty people. I chatted with actors and actresses, movie directors, and magazine writers. It was fantastic for networking.

People came and went throughout all hours of the night. Everyone who was at the party was pretty loaded. Once I knew all was good and that the people at the house were respectful of the environment, I started to have some drinks, and get into the fun.

On the second floor, there was an area that overlooked the pool which you could access from the master bedroom. There was a spiral staircase which led from this balcony down to the front of the pool. I remember someone jokingly saying how it would be fun to jump off the house and into the pool. Of course, I had to try it! I ran down to the basement and grabbed a pair of swim trunks that I had left at the house. I headed up to the master bedroom. After I changed into my swim trunks, I went out to the patio. To my left was a guardrail. If I stood on it, I could pull myself up on top of the roof.

I was twenty feet off the ground below, if not higher. The distance from the edge of the house to the edge of the pool was maybe fifteen feet from the house. I knew I would have to launch myself off the roof quite far. On top of that, I had to clear the spiral staircase. If I clipped it with any part of my body, it would most likely slow me down enough that I wouldn't clear the pavement between the house and the pool. I am not a mathematician but even I knew, despite being half drunk, the odds were probably not in my favor to actually make the jump.

Word quickly spread that there was a guy who was about to attempt a jump from the rooftop into the pool. Most people were looking up in my direction, so I thought, as one of the hosts, I would take the opportunity to address everyone. I told everyone to raise their glasses in the air so we could give cheers to Noah and wish him even more success in the fashion industry in Vancouver. I said how honored I was and what a pleasure it was working with him and thanked him for all the great times. I then stepped back out of view from the people below, and then walked slowly back into view, again looking down on the crowd. The whole backyard was packed full of people.

I looked down from where I was standing and could see there were people still coming out of the house. I could hear people saying things like, "He is crazy, be careful, don't do it." But I could also hear people saying, "Come on, you can do it! You're the man! Come on, bro!" I stood on the edge of the roof again and threw both hands in the air and yelled out, "Noah, this is for you!" I then stepped back out of view again, about ten feet back, which was enough for me to get some speed before I launched myself off of the roof.

My steps had to be perfect. If I jumped too soon, there was a high chance that I wouldn't make the distance needed to clear the stairs and would probably hurt myself badly on the pavement below. If I had to take a stutter step because I miscalculated distance, I'd also slow down enough that my jump would be compromised, and I would probably crack my skull open. I started with a few stutter steps and hoped that the distance would work out. I sped up and ran until there was no stopping my momentum. This was it. I launched myself off of the roof, head first.

You know how people say when you are in a car accident, things slow down? That was not what happened, at all. It was so fast. When I was in the air, I could see the railing of the stairs. The top half of my body had cleared the stairs, and I realized I had to quickly lift my legs and feet so the bottom half of my body could clear them as well. Once I was clear of the stairwell, my eyes moved to look at the edge of the pool. I landed in the middle of the pool, which wasn't necessarily a bad thing, but it left me less room to stop, and I lightly crashed into the wall on the far side of the pool. The pool was only eight feet deep. I knew that once I touched the water with my hands, I would have to curl my back immediately. If I had gone too deeply into the pool, I would have easily broken my neck.

When I entered the water, I felt my shoulder scrape against

the bottom of the pool. I headed back up to the surface quickly, and when I broke through it, I sprung up gasping for breath. I could hear everyone yelling and cheering that I was okay. It was an amazing rush!

I really don't know what I was thinking — or if I was really thinking at all. Once the idea entered my head, I lost reason. There was a crowd and I wanted to do something crazy ... even though I knew I could hit the bottom of the pool and be paralyzed or even die. The drugs and alcohol were clouding my judgement

40

NO MEMORY

My life would change again. This time forever.

Noah and I had traveled to Calgary for a fashion gala. We took my purple and grey Eagle Talon, a six-speed turbo sports car. I loved it because it was fast and sporty. Once the gala was over and the partying complete, we began our journey back home to Vancouver.

The posted speed limit was 70 km/hour and the truck ahead of me was only going sixty kilometers. As we approached the truck, I downshifted to fourth gear and started to accelerate around it. What I didn't realize when I tried to pass the truck was that I was going into a long curve on the highway. I hit some pea gravel on the road and lost traction. My car careened into and then almost over the meridian. Soon we would have headed straight into oncoming traffic, eight or more vehicles all travelling at 80 km/hour. Not one of them would have been able to stop or avoid us.

When I initially felt my rear driver side tire hit the meridian, I knew it was now or never, and I cranked my wheel to the right to bring my car back to the right side of the road. The front right side of my bumper hit the road first when we came off the meridian, forcing the rear end of the car to shift left. I had to correct the direction, so

I turned my wheel left, which sent the rear end of my vehicle to the right. We started fishtailing. I knew we were in trouble because we were still travelling fast and were completely out of control.

For a moment, I thought I might get the car back under control, but then I realized we were starting to swing further and further out of control. There was only one way this situation could turn out. Suddenly, we hit dry asphalt and my car shot to the right. We went sideways from left to right lane, ending up directly under the trailer of a semi that was passing by. The rear three sets of tires of the semi came into contact with the front end of the right side of my vehicle. My car was crushed under the tires of the semi and a big steel machine on the back of the semi's trailer hooked into the wheel well of my car and launched my car into the air.

A driver travelling behind me later told me that it was like a scene straight out of a movie. My car was launched nine feet into the air. The front of my car was closest to the road, and the rear end of my car was fifteen feet in the air. My car rotated like a helicopter blade, three full rotations before crashing down. Once we made contact with the ground, my car bounced back up into the air while rotating one hundred eighty degrees. We ended up rolling three times before the car finally came to a stop.

For most of the accident, things felt like they were in slow motion, but when we rolled, I felt nothing but a fast movement. It was almost like I was in fast forward.

The first person on the scene was a woman. She asked me if I was alright and let me know I was in an accident. She said she was a nurse and asked if she could move me. It wasn't long before more people came and assisted her. I was in the crushed vehicle for a while. I was shocked that I was alive. I checked myself for blood and made sure I could feel my legs. The woman, with two men assisting, got me out of the vehicle, being very careful with my neck. About ten minutes had gone by before things really started coming together for me, mentally.

I the background, I could hear people talking about the accident. They talked about how crazy an event it was. Apparently, when my car first made contact with the meridian, it sent a piece of concrete so high into the air that it landed on a truck travelling eight spots back in the traffic behind me, shattering its windshield.

The semi driver had only seen my car airborne in his side mirror and had stopped up the road and walked back to make sure we were okay. The driver didn't even feel the impact. He only saw that I was out of control in the next lane. He didn't even know that we made contact until he saw my car was airborne.

By this time, Noah was out of the vehicle, and I saw that he was shaken up, but thankfully, he was walking and talking. Apparently, from the side of the road, I called my mom and told her that I had been in a terrible accident. I have to take her word for that as I don't remember talking to her or what was said. The nurse stayed with us until an ambulance showed up. The EMTs asked me a series of questions to make sure I knew my name and where I was and so forth. I was amazed that I hadn't broken one bone or had any severe lacerations, even though all the windows were smashed and there was glass everywhere. After we had given our statements to the police, Noah and I were free to go. There was no hospital visit, no trip in the ambulance; we just rented a vehicle and drove back to Vancouver. It was so strange how we had both been in the worst accident of our lives and then acted like it didn't happen.

When I returned to Langley, my back was hurting quite badly. After a couple of weeks, I went to see a doctor. My head also hurt a lot, but I only told the doctor about the accident and complained of severe back pain. He gave me some medication and sent me on my way. At my follow up doctor's appointment weeks later, the doctor asked me the most unusual question. It was a question that a doctor had never asked me before.

"What is your mother's maiden name?"

I remember sitting there and thinking and thinking, but it didn't come to me. It was such an easy question, one that I knew that I knew the answer to. I should have been able to answer that question in an instant. I literally did not remember the answer to the question. I think I was in as much shock as the doctor.

He asked me again, "What is your mother's maiden name? Think real hard."

When I couldn't come up with an answer, his original task of assessing my back became minor in comparison to assessing what was going on with my new-found brain injury. He picked up the phone and booked me in for a CT scan and other tests for the brain. He also booked me tests for my vision and reflex. He continued to ask me many questions, like, "What was my street number back home? What were my family members' names? Who were my friends from back home?" I couldn't answer any of his questions, and suddenly, in an instant, I was lost. I could not believe that I couldn't answer any of these easy questions.

The doctor's office was right across the highway from where I lived in Langley, BC. When it came time to attend these special tests and get my brain scanned, it scared me. It really bothered me that I couldn't remember anything. I was confused and worried. When the tests results came back, the receptionist at the doctor's office called me to book an appointment to go over the results.

When I arrived, I was very nervous and worried. What was going on? What was the doctor going to say to me? I was ushered into an examination room and I sat in a chair with my hands on my knees, trying to remain calm. The doctor entered the room with a rather large envelope in his hands. He made some small talk by asking how my back was and so forth. I am sure he was warming me up for what came next. He reached into the envelope and showed me an image from the CT scan. He had the results on his computer from the other tests. He explained to me that it was quite clear to him that I had long and short-term memory loss from the violent impact of the car accident. He was most worried about the long-term effects, and to be honest, I was too. As I had lost so much of my memory, he thought it would be best if I was around those that knew me throughout my life — my family and friends. He felt that it was 100% necessary to get home to Saskatoon as soon as possible, so I could start trying to put the pieces of my life back together.

I explained to the doctor that I definitely did not have the funds to go home. He asked me for my ID, which was my Saskatchewan driver's license, and he handed it to the receptionist at the front desk and talked to her briefly. I guess when they spoke, she was instructed to book me a flight home. When I left the doctor's office, he mentioned that I would get another call from the office within the next day. The call confirmed that the doctor had actually booked me a trip home. I still do not understand why he bought me that ticket, even to this day. When I stopped in to thank him on the way to the airport on the day I left, his only response to me was, "Go get better and good luck."

A friend Jamison drove me to the airport. It was the strangest feeling. I knew all about my life in Vancouver, but I didn't have a clue where I was going or who I was going to see because of my memory loss. It was an exciting time, in a way, and also an extremely confusing one. I didn't know what to expect. When I got to the airport, I thanked my friend for the ride and shut the door to his car. I did not have a clue where I was going. I mean, I knew I was going to Saskatoon, but where would I end up?

When I landed in Saskatoon, I took a cab from the airport to the address on my driver's license. When I pulled up, I said to myself, "Yep, this must be home." It was one of the strangest feelings ever. Knowing the house was more a feeling, than a true recognition.

I didn't call or announce that I was coming home, as I didn't know any numbers. Which is ironic because I remembered my mom's number well enough to call her from the car accident scene! When I rang the doorbell, my sister Nola, came to the door. She introduced herself, and I walked into the house. I walked into the living room and looked at my mom over as she sat in the chair in the corner, which had a clear view out of the front bay window. I said, "Obviously, that's Mom." The doctor's office must have used the information that I had previously filled out for my emergency contact.

I was a mess. Who was I? Would I ever be able to piece it all together?

Upon hearing that I would be returning to Saskatoon, my mom had planned a big dinner that evening at a relative's restaurant. She asked me if I wanted to attend. I politely said, "No, thanks."

She mentioned that she thought it would be a good idea, as my aunts and uncles and family friends were going to come. I really didn't want to go, as I felt mentally off, but it was an excellent opportunity to meet family, so I ended up going. Upon arriving, I was approached by many people. They all told me that they had known me since I was this little. I felt silly, but I had to tell them about the accident and that I had no idea who they were. There was one lady who grabbed my arm and took me to a table and pointed to everyone in the room. "That is so and so and that is his wife and your aunt and so on." Most people came up to me telling me stories of how I was as a kid.

41

WORKING HARD AND PARTYING HARDER

I decided to take a job at a construction camp in Alberta. My supervisor's name was David. He was a young supervisor, but he knew what he was doing and we got along well. I was put in a trailer with David and another man named Ryan, who was the backhoe operator.

The backhoe was the machine that dug a trench as we laid the pipe in the ground. Our bulldozer operator's name was Gordon and you didn't want to piss him off. He was one of those tough guys, but we were buds. I was friends with a few other guys from the crew, Devon and CJ. We had a solid crew.

Our days started early. We had to be on the job site at 6:00 a.m. to fire up the machines. There was always a brief meeting in the morning where we went over safety regulations and made sure that everyone was aware of the safety hazards and what to do in the event of a workplace incident.

We worked ten hours per day on average. This was a tough job. You had to know how to shovel because that was basically what we did all day. The pipe we were using was a sixteen-inch cast iron pipe, which is a heavy-duty pipe. We would rig up the pipe using lifting straps and lay it out near the top by the highway, from male end to female ends, so it was prepped and ready to go when we needed it. Our one-day record was seventy-three lengths of pipe in the ground. On most days, we averaged anywhere from forty to fifty pipes. Some days, we would hit different types of ground, and when it was rocky, things slowed down. On those days, it wasn't frowned upon if we only placed forty pipes in the ground.

My childhood friend, Robyn, had moved to Calgary and lived not too far from my construction job. We decided to meet up. We went to the local pub where our crew all hung out after work. Robyn and I sat and shared stories and played some pool. After the bar, Robyn and I snuck into my room, which was in trailer I shared with Ryan and Gordon. Robyn cuddled up close to me to get warm. Cuddling was nice, but the kiss that came after was even nicer.

I was shocked because there had been so many years where we were not romantically involved. At the time, I wasn't expecting to be lip-locked with my childhood best girlfriend. It wasn't soon after the kiss that things really started to heat up. I could feel the intensity growing between us, and I knew that it wouldn't be long before the aggressive kissing and touching would inevitably lead to something more. I had always wanted this to happen with her. The clothes started to come off, and I climbed on top of her. She made a little remark about keeping the heat under the blanket.

We were kissing and grinding and grabbing and sucking, and it all got very intense. The build-up was crazy. Then, everything stopped—including breathing. I mean, everything stopped. I remember looking down at Robyn, and she was looking up at me. I asked her if she was sure she wanted to do this, and she asked if I was sure about continuing. It was obvious we both were considerate of how the other felt. I think we both realized that at this moment a couple of things could happen. We could have sex and end our friendship because it would make things weird, or we could continue and feel happy we shared something so beautiful with someone we cared about deeply.

We started off slow. I felt the passion was there; eventually, things got even more intense, and we both climaxed. I collapsed onto her, and we just lay there and talked. The next morning, she got up and drove back to Calgary.

The great thing was that nothing weird came out of that and we remained close friends. Many women had come into my life and I had many intimate relationships, some short and some longer. Looking back now, I realize how confused I was about relationships and sex and how that was tied to the sexual abuse I experienced when I was younger.

42

OPPORTUNITIES GAINED AND LOST

In 2008, I received another call from Noah. He was again asking me to come back and work with him in fashion. This time he had an opportunity to do a grand opening for an upscale nightclub located in the West Edmonton Mall. The pay was extremely good. $2,000 per week to help promote and organize the event. I was never one to be scared of change, and if there was an opportunity, I was in, with no questions asked. So, off to Edmonton I went to meet up with Noah.

During the planning period and event, I met many great people. I was thrown right into the fire. As plans grew, there were some disagreements between Noah and the owners, who did not like the direction Noah was headed. One week before the grand opening, there was a large disagreement between Noah and the owners. He wanted to open the show by presenting himself tied to a burning cross. (Noah was always an extremist. He liked to push the limits, and I was open to his ideas, but this sounded a tad crazy even to me.) This disagreement became an impasse, and Noah packed his bags. He told me we were to head back to Vancouver, but I responded that I wasn't going to join him. I had built a relationship with the owners and I was staying to finish planning the opening. I had met a lot of great people and I wanted to stay and complete the project. So, Noah went, and I stayed.

We were to use Noah's clothing for the opening fashion gala, but that was no longer an option. I went from promoting to planning, hustling to find stores that would partake in the event and that wanted to display their clothing in the show. I knew that Noah had talked to salon owner, Danica, who was putting on a hair show as part of the opening. I went to her first and made sure she was still on board. In addition to the clothing, I had to find models and coordinate the entire fashion show — within a week. During this process, I met Christian, who became a good friend. I was looking for male models, and I walked past Christian and thought that he sure fit the profile. He was tall, built, had blonde hair, a great jawline, and golden-bronzed skin. Guys were less likely than women to try modelling, and when I first approached Christian, his first reaction was a definite no. Later in the day, I bumped into him again in a different part of the mall, and he was more open to the idea. I gave him my card and set up some fittings for him.

As well as rehearsals, fittings, and promotion, many other things needed attention. The whole show needed final planning — setting the timing, music, steps, and lighting; backstage prep and makeup; and coordination of the various acts and little shows that would be part of the gala. It all needed to happen in a short time.

In the end, it all came together and the show was a huge success! Sold out and packed. It was wonderful to see everyone's hard work pay off!

After the grand opening, the owner of the nightclub asked if I wanted to stay and work at the club. As part of the offer, I could stay at his place. I would work weekends as a bartender and do promotions during the week. I agreed and soon my job evolved beyond bartending and into the role of VIP Service Manager. This role opened new doors for networking, and because I always took care of the VIPs, I was well-liked by many. My duties involved calling people and booking the tables for bottle service.

It sounded and was a wonderful opportunity. Great job, nice accommodation. All I had to do was not to do drugs in the house.

But it didn't take long before my addictions overpowered my train of thought and I was asked to move out.

It seemed like the partying never stopped. Canada Day weekend 2008, I headed for a houseboat trip in the beautiful Shuswaps of B.C with a group of friends. While there, I met a beautiful person named Alyssa. Throughout the trip, we had some real talks, so the groundwork was laid for a possible relationship in Edmonton, where both she and I lived at the time. We first reconnected by phone and then started to visit and spend a bit more time with one another before we actually started to date. Our conversations were sincere and heartfelt, which I enjoyed. Alyssa lived in a townhouse and had two great dogs. We enjoyed taking the dogs for walks and watching movies. Alyssa was more than a pretty face, she had a gentle but realistic heart, and she was confident and authentic. It was amazing to share a deep connection with her.

But I was still living the party life and it was clear that she didn't want to be deeply involved with a guy who always partied. Eventually, she called it off. It was clear that I didn't have too much to offer her. I didn't have a great job and or stable funds, so why would she stay with me? She wanted a family, and I was far away from being ready for that.

Alyssa and I still talk today. She has two beautiful children and is doing her thing. I often find myself reflecting on our times together, mostly because we never argued or fought. Our timing was just off. Alyssa is fantastic, and she deserves to have an amazing man take care of her and her two little guys. I always want the best for her.

When I returned from the Shuswap, my focus had turned to my friend, Tyler, who was set to get married later that month in Saskatchewan. I had no more vacation time left and the club in Edmonton would not allow me the time off to attend the wedding. However, there was nothing that would stop me from attending my friend wedding — especially as I was to be a groomsman. As a result, I eventually chose to leave my job at the club in Edmonton.

I was in peak shape weighing in at 217 pounds and I was eager to see, and be seen by, good friends who I hadn't seen in years. When I arrived for the suit fitting, Tyler and the other groomsmen were getting fitted. I remember feeling like time hadn't moved on at all from when we all hung out together.

43

SURGERIES AND HOPE

When I met first locked eyes with Claire, there was an instant attraction. She was always smiling and had a glowing energy about her. Did I know then that I would fall madly in love with her? No way, no chance.

Funnily enough, after we met, we learned that we lived only three blocks away from each other. I remember our conversation on the phone when she explained to me where she lived. I joked that I could throw a rock and hit her house from where I lived. We had a connection which is hard for me to explain.

Claire was pure love and endlessly cared about people. Her energy of love for people in her life flowed like a stream of fresh water from a mountain. Everyone loved her too, and she was, for the most part, always smiling, even when times were tough. We had deeply emotional times together, and I'll never forget the love she showed me.

But we both struggled with drug abuse, which ultimately brought about the death of our relationship.

My car accidents had left me in rough shape. My back pain was not getting better. Wincing in pain most hours of the day, I was heavily medicated with Oxycodone, Morphine, and other narcotics in addition to my "non-prescribed" drug use.

Surgery seemed like the logical outlet even though I knew that would be a huge risk. My back specialist in Saskatoon agreed, expressing the dangers of the surgery to me clearly. He pulled up my MRI images and x-rays on the computer screen and explained what was causing the immense pain that kept me crippled most of the time. On my last visit to his office, he asked, "Niall, are you sure you want to go through this operation? There is a 50/50 chance you will never walk again."

I replied, "Whatever takes the pain away."

He brought out a paper for me to sign that stated that if anything were to go wrong during the surgery that he would not be held liable and that I could not sue him. It gives you an idea of just how bad the pain really was that I signed the document with no hesitation. I took the chance and had the surgery knowing full well I may never walk again.

Claire was there for me during this time. After the surgery she took great care of me. I am forever thankful that she was by my side. I cannot imagine that it was easy for her. She worked at a radio station downtown and she was doing well in her career. I know she took the time to come from her job and give me my medication. Sometimes she made me a bite to eat, and if she wasn't able to, her mom helped out.

The recovery time after the surgery was a blur. I was between a waking and sleeping state. I woke in a sweat, took my meds, and then crashed. This cycle went on for well over three weeks. Claire really blessed me with the care she gave. Whether it was helping me go to the bathroom, helping me with food or meds, or helping me get up, I couldn't function without her assistance.

Claire struggled constantly with her weight. She did these super intense weight-loss diets and then put the weight back on. She would fluctuate off and on like repeatedly.

One day, we were downstairs at her house and she suddenly broke down and started to bawl. I am not sure what made her cry so hard at that moment, but I felt her pain. That moment really hurt my heart. Her mom and I told her that she was fine the way she was and brushed away her tears. We told her to let go of the mindset that she was fat. I wasn't concerned about Claire's weight and it was horrible to see her happy and loving spirit thrown aside. She was in such pain.

My memories of our good times together reverberates still today. Every time the song Patience by Guns & Roses comes on, I recall the time I sang to her at a karaoke bar in Saskatoon. I loved to sing that song to her. Claire and I always had fun at the karaoke bar. We sang, danced, and socialized like there was no tomorrow. It was what we did best together.

But sadly, for every bright side, there is a dark side. Claire and I both struggled with alcohol and drug abuse. We used it as an outlet for whatever our needs were. We found a joy in it that wasn't practical or healthy. On a typical night, we went out for drinks and got messed up, and then stepped it up with some cocaine or MDMA — or whatever we could get our hands on. Claire and I never had to look far to get what we wanted. We both knew the entire city and had connections.

Near the end of our relationship, we made several attempts to stop partying. Booze was killing our relationship, along with the mix of drugs. It was a lose-lose situation. We were both aware of the damage we were doing to ourselves and to one another, but we couldn't stop.

One day I told Claire that if our relationship was going to work, we would have to stop partying. I said that I was willing to do whatever it took to get better. I wanted to do anything to stop destroying our love. I remember sitting in the car and asking her one last time if we should give up the drugs and the booze.

Her reply was, "No."

I gave her a kiss and said goodbye to her right then and there and walked into my house.

My response may sound extreme, but that was the way it had to happen. My heart was broken again, but I knew I had to get rid of this toxic relationship, regardless of what my heart told me.

It was not long before I was almost bedridden. I needed to get to a back specialist and see what was happening.

Claire had come by my mom's house and we talked for a long time. She told me that she was okay with all that had happened between us. We agreed that we would hang out like friends and to me that felt terrific. Claire insisted on taking me to the doctor. I know in my heart that she knew something was up and only cared that I took care of myself.

After a series of tests and questions, Claire and I sat in the doctor's office awaiting news about my condition. I was scared and nervous. I knew it wasn't going to be good news. Claire and I discussed what a second surgery might mean. I didn't even have to ask her if she would help me in the way she helped me through the first surgery. She made it clear that regardless of whether or not we were together, she wanted to do what she could to help me through the recovery period.

The doctor walked in and asked about my pain. He asked me to grade it on a scale of one to ten, with ten being the greatest pain and one being the least in the amount of pain. I said I was at level nine because the pain was excruciating all the time. The doctor told me that I needed to have surgery, and he again stressed that there was a 50/50 chance that I may not walk again afterward.

I said I was willing to take that chance as I couldn't bear the pain.

My mom moved me into the main floor of the house. I stayed in Amber's old room, which allowed me to be next to the bathroom. Claire made sure I took my medications as directed. She sometimes cuddled up next to me, and we watched movies. I can't emphasize enough how important it was that Claire helped me through these two tough surgeries. She is an amazing woman, and I am glad to know she is happy living with her partner. I sometimes think of her and can only grin. The footprint she left in my heart is a warmly felt smile.

44

HEALED

My back surgery had only been partially successful. I continued to struggle with pain that would often cause me to drop to the floor. I had asked for my job back at the nightclub once I returned to Edmonton, but even the basic activities were challenging.

At the nightclub, a coworker named Dina and I worked together to promote the bar by delivering flyers in the surrounding neighborhood. One night, Dina received a phone call from her mom, who suggested that there was an event that she thought we should attend. There was a healer who heals through the name of Jesus. He had travelled all over the world, healing many people from various diseases and physical disabilities.

Dina and I both laughed and chuckled to one another and carried on our merry way, delivering the promotion flyers. About thirty minutes later, Dina received another call from her mom; this time with a real urgency that she and I attend this event. Dina half-jokingly asked if I wanted to go check this guy out. My first response was that I didn't believe in that healing stuff. I had seen it on TV and couldn't wrap my head around the idea that it was even possible;

however, in the end, we agreed to check it out, and if we weren't feeling it, we decided we would just leave.

When we arrived, I slowly pulled myself from the jeep, wincing in pain. We walked in and took our seats among the many people who were already seated. It wasn't long before the speaker came out and explained a little about who he was. He said that through the name of Jesus, he could heal. I still couldn't wrap my brain around this healing idea, but I decided to observe anyway. One by one, I watched as people of various ages went up front, looking to be healed. To my amazement, they all seemed to return to their seats restored. I remember thinking: What a great hoax! He must have contracted these people ahead of time.

After the last person sat back down, he asked, "Is there anyone else in the crowd that wants to be healed?"

Dina jabbed me sharply in the side, motioning for me to go up.

"No way," I said.

"Just go!"

"Fine," I said, thinking that I would just go to amuse her.

Although I was in pain, I tried my best to walk without limping. As I neared the stage, the speaker asked me to sit in a chair. Then he sat in a chair across from me. He started to pray in the name of Jesus to allow his healing hand to come over him and allow him to once again perform healing through the name of Jesus.

I was trying very hard not to laugh but was able to keep it together. As we sat across from one another, he looked me straight in the eyes and said he could see the pain in me. He asked me to straighten one of my legs out to him. He grabbed the back of my straightened leg, just above my heel. Once he had a hold of the one leg, he asked for the other one. He showed me that when my legs were side by side, one was about an inch longer.

He started praying for the muscles in the area to return to their proper form. He asked Jesus to align my spine and to allow me to be free of the pain. He spoke of blood pumping into the area and how he could see it helping my circulation.

He didn't pull or twist my legs. As I lowered both my legs to the ground, he continued to pray. I was no longer laughing inside because I could feel a warming in my lower back where the pain resonated from. Inside my body, I could clearly feel things moving. I was in awe and let the process happen.

When the prayer was completed, the man politely asked me for my left leg and again for the right leg. This time when he put my feet together, my feet were identical in length. He held my feet in the air which gave me a clear view of them, and he then asked me to stand, as I was now healed from the pain.

And so I did. I stood. There was absolutely no pain whatsoever! I moved in ways that I was incapable of moving just ten minutes before. I couldn't grasp how something like this was possible.

"It's the power of Jesus," he said. He advised me that if the pain were to return, I say, "Devil be gone, devil be gone in the name of Jesus, I command you back to the pits of hell."

He reminded me that as long as I kept my faith strong that the devil had no power and couldn't inflict that pain on me again. To this day, this stands to be true. I have felt tightness in my back but never have experienced that sharp pain that was crippling my life, the kind of pain that would compel me to use that phrase, "Devil be gone." It was a true healing miracle in the name of Jesus.

But, as time passed, my back started to hurt again. I decided to return to Saskatoon.

45

TRAUMA ALWAYS WINS

In 2009, five months after the surgery, I was feeling well enough to once more undertake physical work. I got a job working for a construction company. I was part of a crew working on a building on the east side of Saskatoon. On this job, I met some solid friends like Bruce, Larry, and Gavin. Bruce and Larry were steel framers, and I ran a mobile crane.

This was an interesting job for me with definite challenges. One challenge was dealing with the wind when lifting up a prefabricated wall. The goal was to land the wall on a set of chalked parallel lines drawn on a concrete slab. Another fun challenge was lifting windows. They were relatively large, and when lifting them around a building, if the wind hit them, they started to spin like a top. It was very dangerous. When this happened, the goal was either to get the load down on the ground or to get it to where it needed to land in the building as fast as possible. The job took a certain amount of skill.

I wasn't always running a crane. Gavin was the primary crane operator on this job, and I was the backup. When he was called to do something else, I would take over. Otherwise, I did steel framing, which I learned on the job. I had some great journeymen that taught me how to frame, fabricate, and work with steel (all skills that served me well years later when I worked with another steel framing company).

After I joined the crew, I clicked with Bruce, Larry, and Gavin quickly, hanging out outside of work as well as on the job. When it came to being bad-asses, we were all on the same page. Bruce and Gavin were the worst. They were tattooed up and knew the wrong types of people. We all had connections who could make things go badly for someone. (One thing that was neat about this job was that there was a guy who knew my brother. He was a supervisor; they had played hockey together. I always seemed to bump into people who knew Cyril. It was nice because I loved to hear stories about him.)

On a cold Wednesday, our crew lost a friend, and a mother and father lost a son. I had pulled a double shift and once home, I hit the bed and crashed. When I woke up, I noticed my work had called. I called back and was given the horrible news. One of our employees hadn't tied himself off and plummeted from the sixth story of the elevator shaft. He landed on another co-worker who was picking something up off of the ground. This co-worker wasn't looking up at the time, and was crushed by the impact. One crew member died, and another had a broken back. We felt the effects of the incident heavily.

They say life travels in circles and repeats itself. That certainly seemed to be true for me. The trauma of my co-worker's death was painful and I soon fell right back down the rabbit hole with trouble waiting at the bottom.

I felt like I was in a perpetual circular loop. Once I reconnected with my old friends, it became easy for me to get a hold of drugs. I was working hard in the various jobs I had, and during the week I was somewhat responsible. But come the weekends, it was on, full speed ahead. I gathered with my boys, and we would get drugs and booze. We often would meet at the house of my buddy, Trey, and we would make the call for the treats, making sure we all had enough to sustain us through the night. I went to various bars and pubs, and if I saw someone I knew, and I knew they enjoyed doing the odd rip, I would invite them for a line or two.

When others had drugs, and I didn't, hooking people up was a part of the mutual understanding between all the people who used the drug. After the bar, we would gather up a small group of people and be sure to all grab more product and drink and then socialize. Sometimes, we would hook up with random people that we met that night at the bar. Everyone was always very open to meeting new people. It was always the case that somehow, some way, the new people of the group knew someone indirectly. Stories would be told and we would all laugh, continuing to have a blast until the early morning hours of the next day. By the time all the booze and drugs were gone, we would all go for breakfast and then go our separate ways. A phone call would come that next evening making plans and a repeat night would be in order.

I lost many people from my life early. More deaths than most people my age, and usually due to drugs and bad decisions. And all of those losses left a trauma, a wound needing to be healed.

Like Pam.

I first met Pam back in Grade 3. The first time I laid eyes on her, she was walking into the classroom and looking over at me and smiling. It was a very special moment in time for me. Pam always had a radiant smile. She and I had kept in touch on and off again over the years. Even though we never had a close relationship, we continued to have a deep respect for each other.

I met up one night with Pam. It was unexpected, but we ended up sleeping together. I remember the first time our lips touched. It was a moment that I had always thought about. I was in complete shock because I always believed that she just wasn't ever attracted to me. For me, it was totally insane; it felt like I poured out all the emotions that had built up from years and years of crushing on her.

When I learned of her death, flashes of memories poured into my thoughts and reflections from our childhood surfaced. One day, Pam and I were walking in an alleyway. There was a glass window propped up in the alley and I decided it would be a good idea if I kicked the glass out from the window frame. When I did this, a lady, who was in her backyard, came out and said, "You better run Peanut Butter!"

Pam and I both fled the scene. We laughed for years about that incident. Sometimes when she messaged me, she would close off her message with, "Love Ya Peanut Butter."

Pam was a special person to me, and our friendship will always be dear to my heart. Unfortunately, she also struggled with addictions and drugs ultimately took her life.

46

MINING

My friends, Miles and Trey, both worked at a potash mine near Saskatoon and on my behalf, Trey called the owner of a contract mining company that worked at the various potash mines around Saskatchewan and asked if he was hiring. Shortly after, I received a call from one of the supervisors of the crews that went underground at the mine.

Just after I started, I met Nolan, the owner of the company. In talking with him, I found out that Nolan was married to the girl who gave me my first kiss, Hailey. Hailey had always been attractive, even when we were kids. Everyone told me Nolan was a real screamer when someone messed up, so I tried hard not to screw up. I wasn't going to let anyone see that I wasn't working as hard or harder than anyone else, especially with having a history of friendship with the owner's wife.

Most of the guys thought I was just some pretty boy, but I quickly proved that I was there to work. I didn't mind the harsh environment and would try to finish whatever task I was assigned. Even though the conditions 1300 meters underground were hot, I really enjoyed the job, especially the physical aspect of it.

I liked working with the air-powered machine (the stopper), driving support bolts into the ceiling. As I recall, we were using seventeen-foot bolts, each that could hold 1000 pounds. These bolts looked like a thick type of rebar. One man worked the stopper, and another one put the resin in the drilled hole. The amount of resin depended on the depth we were drilling into the rock formation. When we grabbed the drill bit, it was hot—as it was coming back out of a hole that was just drilled.

We also used a smaller tool, a mini hammer drill. We had to take shifts using it as we could only work ten to fifteen minutes at a time before our arms burned and we felt too weak to hold the tool. We worked off of scaffolding. That was all we did for months on end. It was brutal work.

Nolan's contract company was a great outfit to work for, but I quit to take a union job at another mine, thinking it promised more opportunity for the future. As soon as I started with my new company, I saw that everything was different. The guys on the crew barely worked. They sat around, played cards, read magazines, and had naps. They did as little as possible and were paid well. I was in shock. It was so different from the culture of hard work that I was used to. I was taught to work hard, and when I applied that ethic with the new guys, I was told to quit trying to be a hero.

Although I did learn a lot at this job, the fun in the work was lost. The mining industry didn't appeal to me any longer. I tried to get back on with Nolan's company, but they were going through cutbacks and had no room for extra staff. I left the mining industry to take a construction job building the new police station in Saskatoon.

I had not lost interest in keeping myself fit, nor had I lost interest in pursuing a modelling career. I went back to the gym I had once belonged to in Saskatoon and started a routine of strict eating and fitness. Although I always struggled with back pain, there wasn't much else that could stop me from achieving my fitness goals.

The gym opened at 5:00 a.m. and closed at 11:00 p.m., which were perfect hours to complement my work schedules. I worked 7:00 a.m. to 7:00 p.m. for a week and then had a 24-hour shift before my work schedule switched to reverse hours from 7:00 p.m. to 7:00 a.m. I worked two weeks on and one week off. I worked out relentlessly and followed the instructions of my coach. Discipline was a must, and I knew it. I think it was hard for a lot of my friends to understand why I was so intensely focused, but I had a clear vision and stopped at nothing to achieve it.

47

PEPPER EVENTS

Deep inside, I still wanted to do something that I was passionate about. I felt I was wasting my time working in construction. Even though I wasn't in Vancouver, I started looking for opportunities to get back into fashion, perhaps in the local fashion industry in Saskatoon.

I started working as an event planner for a nightclub known as Bailey's on the east side of Saskatoon. My first show with them was "The Rock and Roll Fashion Gala." When it came to planning shows, I had a pretty impressive track record. Vancouver and Edmonton had sold-out shows. That past success extended to Saskatoon. I presented a couple more shows with the nightclub, but I wasn't really making anyone money except the bar owners. I decided I would try it on my own.

I started my own company, called Pepper Events. Why the name Pepper? I branded myself as Pepper Fox when I began modelling in Vancouver. When I went to Edmonton, I was also called Pepper. It's kind of a hard name to forget, and it is a name that most drunk or high people can likely remember. The name Pepper went viral in the fashion/bar industry. When I first came back home to Saskatoon, I let my friends and family know that I had been branding myself under the name Pepper Fox. Everyone began to call me Pepper. Years later, my best friends still call me Pepper or Peps. I have been in different cities where a shout will ring out from within a crowd, "Pepper!" When that happens, I know the person calling my name is an old friend from back home or from one of the many cities I have lived in.

So, starting a company called Pepper Events made sense. Creating the company was the first step in my doing what I was best at, something that I was passionate about.

After "The Rock and Roll Fashion Gala," I was on a roll in Saskatoon. I met a guy named Connor, who owned a store with his wife located in downtown Saskatoon. Connor's store carried some brands that were not in any other stores in the city. They were unique. I would stop in his store every now and then and suggest that they do a fashion show to help get their clothes in front of potential customers. They hadn't done anything like that before and were hesitant. In the course of our conversations, I learned that they had exclusive rights to carry a clothing line called L.A.M.B. which is a fashion collection from Gwen Stefani that features shoes, handbags, and clothing. When I learned about their exclusive relationship to carry this line, a light went on in my head. I proposed that they do a fashion show featuring L.A.M.B. We agreed that I would attempt to make contact with Gwen Stefani's manager to negotiate permission to do a fashion gala featuring her clothing designs.

When I reached Stefani's manager, I cited my experience in the fashion industry, that I was a huge fan of hers in general, and how it would be a tremendous honor to feature her line. A few weeks after our first conversation, he let me know that Gwen had approved the idea as long as her line was properly represented. I shared some video footage of past fashion galas that I had coordinated, and Gwen's manager was pleased and agreed to move forward.

I went back to Connor and let him know that we had the green light and that this event was going to be great. We decided to make this fashion gala a fundraising event. I talked with Wired, a newer radio station in the city, about donating some ad time. After they agreed, I contacted Gwen's manager to see if Gwen would record a plug and send it to the radio station. It was a long shot, but I continued to try, writing a second email asking if Gwen would record a plug.

My long shot became a reality. She recorded something along the lines of, "Hey, this is Gwen Stefani, the designer of L.A.M.B. I am glad to announce that Pepper, with Pepper Events, will be showcasing my designs in your city soon. Thank you all for your support, and I hope you enjoy the fashion gala. Thanks, Pepper!" It may have been short, but I can't think of another person that I knew who could reach out and pull something like that off. I was proud that I accomplished that. When I told Connor the news, he was excited, and we continued moving forward. The gala was a huge success and we raised a lot of money for a non-profit.

In 2012, after the fashion gala with Connor, I turned my attention to another event. My friend Ryan was a liquor rep promoting a brand of vodka imported from Russia. Although Ryan was the rep for this liquor, he had no promotional material or budget for publicity. So, I took things into my own hands and started planning. I didn't have a team working for me. I was solo. I ended up creating and promoting an event myself. I did exactly what I had learned to do in Edmonton and Vancouver, except I was a one-man army. I designed the format of the event and got down to work.

I reached out to a talented filmographer and we met up a few times to make sure we were on the same page regarding what I wanted captured during the event. I also contacted a photographer and discussed photography concepts. We decided that she would have her own area in the event where people could get their pictures taken together with a professional backdrop featuring my logo. Finally, I rented a room at the Exhibition grounds that would fit 1,000 people.

I needed to create a draw for the event, so I went to talented local bands and hired them. I hired my friend, Colten, who did an amazing fire show and several burlesque dancers for onstage entertainment. Then I contracted a stage to be built to accommodate the entertainment.

I still needed to tie a theme to the event. As Russian vodka was the product, I decided to give it a Russian theme, calling it "The Tzars Russian Extravaganza."

With all this going on, I knew that I wouldn't have the time to fully promote the event, so I went to the local radio station Rock

102. They were always at every event in the city, and I knew that if they were involved in some way, they could help draw a crowd. I brought them aboard, and they agreed to do a live broadcast on location as well as MC the event.

Next, I went out and scouted for promotional girls who would be dressed in Pepper Event gear and would walk around with the filmographer, interviewing people to get testimonials of what they thought about the event and the new vodka product. I booked a talented hairdresser for hair and makeup so the promotional girls would look elegant and sexy. I knew that Saskatoon had never seen a show like this before so it would be fresh and would capture the audience at the event. It was all coming together.

All of this planning was based on a $30,000 budget, which was verbally committed to by a silent partner. Two weeks before the event, my silent partner backed out.

I was faced with a difficult decision. Since I didn't have money or backing, I had two choices. One choice was to quit and cancel the event, and the other choice was to get my butt in gear and sell as many presale tickets as I could. I wasn't about to quit. Many people told me to cancel the event, but I believed I could still pull it off.

The day after I made my choice, I woke up at the crack of dawn and got my hustle on. I knew I would have to work twice as hard to make the event profitable without the sponsorship. I went out and sold tickets. I made enough to pay for the venue and the staging, which were the most important items.

I sold four hundred presale tickets at $35 apiece, which only covered some of the costs of the event. I hoped that walk-up sales would be good, as I needed at least four hundred more people to break even. I did everything in my power, used all of my skills, and put in all of my heart to make this event happen.

It was a great event, but I only sold another hundred tickets in walk-up sales. Although this was a reasonable outcome, I lost money on the event and some of the talent and entertainment didn't get paid. It put me in a real rough spot, and I had to shut down Pepper Events. The pulled sponsorship prior to the event crushed me financially. As badly as I wanted to keep it going, I knew that I couldn't. That was the end of Pepper Events. Inc.

48

THE NEEDLE

This failure was tough on me. My inner demons resurfaced and were getting the best of me. It was then that I was given an opportunity to indulge in something I thought I would never do.

I was out getting drunk and looking for cocaine. I was at a small bar on the east side of Saskatoon. I ran into a guy I had seen from time to time. He was an acquaintance really. He pointed out a stranger sitting at a table in a dark corner. I walked to the table and sat down and chatted a bit, mentioning I was looking for product. He mentioned he had some in his room that was attached to the pub.

When we got to his room, he went to the table. I watched curiously as he took out the necessary tools to cook up his cocaine and suck it up into a syringe. The syringe was a new one and, to my relief, he had many new ones still sealed. I watched as he sucked up the liquefied cocaine, placed the tip of the needle to his arm, and inserted it into his vein. When he pressed the syringe's contents into his arm, I cringed.

I was nervous. It was my turn next. We talked for a bit until he was able to catch his bearings from the effects of the drugs. He then proceeded to load a new syringe. He was aware that this would be my first time, so he didn't want to make the shot of cocaine too big, but he also did not want to make it too small.

I was sure whatever size it was going to be, it would do the trick. I have always been vascular enough to see my veins, so I didn't need a tourniquet to make them pop. Then he asked if I was ready.

"Ready as I'll ever get," I replied. I stretched my arm out and watched as he injected the point of the needle into my vein. I was very still as I thought: There is no turning back now.

He pushed the drug into my vein, emptying the contents of the tube of the syringe into my body. He quickly pulled the tip out from my vein, and handed me a little swab, instructing me to hold it on the point where I took the needle tip in my arm.

The rush from the drug was exactly the way I had heard it was. It took action faster and more intensely than anything I had experienced in the past. That was the first and last time I ever did the drug in that manner, but now I know why people enjoy that rush.

I had once met a guy who said he took it with a needle, a manner that I have always been against. He talked about the rush he got off the drug when he "jabbed the vein." Sticking something in my arm had always been my biggest fear, but for some reason that night, I was up for it.

I was a mess, again. My head was full of voices and images. It was in the exact moment when I felt the tip of the needle enter my vein, that I knew I had gone too far. I knew I should seek some sort of help. Of course, I didn't listen to reason and continued to spiral further into my addictions.

49

SHAMBHALA

One night, I had a dream. The vision in the dream was through a video camera panning an area. Suddenly, it panned left and I could see a massive tent with red and white strips. It reminded me of one of those tents you would see at the circus. As the camera panned up and over the tent, a stage appeared, and around the stage were many rocks that were formed into the shape of a square with a distinctive cleared area in the middle. The camera in my dream floated across the front of the stage, allowing me a better look at the staging, lights, and speakers that were on the stage. Then, it continued showing the rocks that were alongside. It eventually panned up once again, back over the tent and zoomed out, showing the total area.

Shortly after, in my desperate search for something to ease what was going on inside my head, I called a guy I had met in Edmonton. His name was Don. He invited me to attend a music festival called Shambhala with a group of his friends.

Shambhala was a five-day festival held on private land near Nelson, BC where drug usage at the event was extreme. The group I was with had an abundance of various drugs, and if we ran out there was an ample supply to be sourced from people walking around the festival, shouting what they had — it would be easy to reload if we needed to. Our group didn't have a supply problem.

When we arrived at the location of the event, we had to set up shop for the night and wait in line for the gates to open. Even though the event hadn't started yet, we all partied while waiting in line to get in. There were people on top of their trailers and motorhomes. We were in a maze of cars and campers, getting the party started a bit early. Shambhala is where I consumed the most drugs I have ever consumed at one time.

We entered the ticket area and walked down a long and narrow dirt road which had signs reading, "Welcome." We turned left down a well-worn path that many vehicles had travelled on, looking for a spot to set up our camper and home base for the event. We found a perfect place that was a city block from the front gate.

Once our tents were set up, and our beds made, the party began. We started with drinks, even though we were not allowed drinks in the festival music area. We snuck ours in and, believe me when I say, we were not the only ones. The first night was relatively tame as we all worked our way into full party mode and awaited the start of the festival the next day. My friend, Christian, reminded me that I should take it easy because we had many days ahead of us. But when it came to partying, I only had one speed, and that was full-steam ahead. Christian knew me too well.

The next morning, as I walked towards the festival stage area, I came to an open area which, to my amazement, had a huge tent. The canopy had thick red and white stripes. As I proceeded further, I saw a rock border in the shape of a square. At the front of the rocks was a stage. We were in an area called the "Rock Pit," one of the many stages of the festival. This was the place I saw in my dream! This blew my mind. I told my friend, and he was in disbelief. When I looked deeply into the area, a shudder ran up and down my body. The only time I had experienced something like this was when I was on that acid trip in Calgary and had the vision of Cyril's accident.

The weather was beautiful, and the sun was shining hot, without a cloud in the sky. I left the camp to go on a journey, ending up at a river stream that flowed beside one of the stages. Massive numbers of people had already gathered. I spotted a few I had known in

Edmonton. It was amazing to see these old friends from the past and to be able to catch up with them and spend some time sitting along the river and consuming. To give you a better idea of what a long list of drugs we had as a group, it would go something like this: cocaine, speed, MDMA, mushrooms, booze, acid, weed, special K, and ecstasy pressed pills. Throughout the day, we had many different mixtures. We knew that if we were not careful of what we were taking, it could escalate badly and turn fatal. I was with friends that I knew I could rely on if anything went wrong. There was also a small medic station set up, in case of instances of overdose.

Shambhala was a real eye-opener for me. I left with a new view on life. The amount of love and positivity that I encountered from attending this event is high-minded, no pun intended. People were kind and everyone, in passing, instead of a regular "Hello" that you might receive in the street, smiled and greeted you with "Happy Sham." The vibe was by far the most positive feeling that I had encountered to this point in my life. Our group had loads of funky costumes, and many of us would walk around in bright body paint, headbands, tight short briefs, and cargo army attire. We walked from stage area to stage area, enjoying the spectacular light and laser shows, letting the music grab us as we danced into the early morning hours.

Once in a while, we would meet to chill out where we had parked the trailer and set up our tents. For the most part, I was loving the river and playing in the hot sun. Of course, I was careful to stay hydrated; although sometimes I would forget, and a friend would come up to me and say, "Here, Pepper, you need water." I was with great friends; friends that looked after one another and made sure everyone was safe.

I had barely slept by day four, and Christian suggested that I get some rest. He pointed out that the last night was always the greatest, and I should be well-rested for it. The DJs were all talented and capable of getting the huge crowds pumped up. Everyone was dancing or jumping in the air with their glow sticks or hula hoops; there were some incredibly talented dancers. I believe by the end of it all, there were just over 19,000 people who attended this event.

I met so many great people from many different areas of the world, some of whom I am still friends with today.

When I finally returned home to Saskatoon, I retired to my room and laid in bed for the rest of the evening. I was hoping to sleep off the existing drugs that were still lingering in my system.

On the Sunday following my return home, I went with my sister to meet up with my parents for dinner at McDonalds. When my sister and I arrived, my parents were already sitting down, and we went to join them. Although I didn't have my appetite back in full swing yet, I got up and ordered a hamburger. When I returned to the table with my food, I sat down and started a conversation with my parents and sister. Suddenly a sharp pain pierced my chest. I grabbed my chest and hunched over in pain.

Am I having a heart attack? Then I comforted myself with the thought: No, I am too young for such a thing to happen. I had just endured the partaking of a rather large amount of drugs. This pain could be a reaction from all the drugs I had over the last five days at Shambhala.

As I sat up, my sister asked what just happened.

"I don't know exactly what that was, but it hurt," I said. I sat up and took some breaths, and again experienced a piercing pain in the exact same area. I grabbed my chest again, and I calmly mentioned to her that I thought she should drive me to the City Hospital, which was reasonably close.

She dropped me off at the emergency doors, and I told her that I would call her when I was done. When I walked in, the nurse asked what I was there for, and I said that I was experiencing sharp pains in my chest. There was no time lost. She took some brief info from me and sent me away to a room. I was given baby aspirin and told by the nurse that a doctor would be in shortly.

As I lay there, a storm of thoughts rushed through my head. Is this going to be it? Did I finally push it too far? Had I overdone it? There was some fear, but I would wait to see what the Doctor had to say.

Before he was able to say anything, I told him where I had been and what I took when it came to the various drugs. He said that my heart was struggling and called the nurse into the room. He told her to get the defibrillator. He placed two square patches on two different spots on my chest. He explained that he would shock me, in the hope that my heart would go back to the way it was supposed to be working. The thought of having an electric shock run through my body really didn't appeal to me, but it's not like the doctor was taking his time at this point. He asked me if I was ready, and I replied, "Ready as I will ever be." A defibrillator shock, if you're wide awake, definitely hurts. It's like being kicked by a mule in the chest.

After the shock, he checked my heartbeat and said it seemed a lot better. He instructed me to lay back and rest for thirty minutes. When he returned, he checked my heart rate and followed up by explaining to me what had just happened. I had a minor heart attack and the attack made my heart beat irregularly — that was what was causing the discomforting pain I had felt. He suggested that I take a break from the drugs for a while or maybe even forever.

You would think that I would have taken his advice. No, not me. I went out and grabbed a couple of grams and got ripped, which was incredibly stupid of me after going through the experience I just had. That is the power of drugs and the weakness of the one who uses them.

50

ANOTHER INJURY

I was working on a job in Calgary for Bruce's company when disaster struck.

I was lifting a window, a large window, when I heard a loud pop. Bruce, who was helping to lift the window, heard the pop too.

We set the window down for a second, and then picked it up again. I immediately had to put it back down. I took off my jacket and my tool belt and harness. When I lifted my shirt and looked, I could clearly tell something was wrong. It hurt for me to breathe, and something was protruding out from my sternum. My sternum had popped out of my chest, and my abdominals had separated from my rib cage.

I went to the emergency room, and was told that my sternum had separated and come loose. Only time could heal it. I could have had surgery, but It would have left a nasty scar. I couldn't return to work due to my injury, and I needed physiotherapy.

I started a return-to-work recovery program through my Workers Compensation claim. The program allowed me to slowly work my way back towards full work duties. I took it easy and tried not to push it. I really wanted the injury to heal, but every time I picked up a steel stud, I could feel my injury pull apart. It was really frustrating. As my physio treatments were ending, Bruce was pushing me to get back to my full duties. Obviously, he didn't want higher Worker Compensation Board (W.C.B.) premiums.

It was then that my buddy, Tyler, from Saskatoon contacted me asking if I wanted to come aboard his new company. He had started his own telecommunications company in Saskatoon. I was pretty excited about this job opportunity because I knew that, first, I would work hard, and second, I had natural skills for the role. Tyler needed an opener, which is a guy who can walk into a business, inquire about their current telecommunication uses, and at a later date, book a meeting with that company. Along with the opener role, I could help with the installs because of my background in construction. Thirdly, I wanted to be back home.

I moved back to Saskatoon and started working with Tyler. We made a great team. It was always nice to hear that Tyler was happy with my performance. I wanted to be a part of Tyler's success by doing a great job for him. I excelled at opening quickly and made some decent sales.

At this time, my back was causing me massive problems. I was on a medication called Gabapentin; a medication to ease the nerve pain from my back. This medication really messed me up. When I abruptly tried to stop the drug, it sent me into a downward spiral. My thoughts were scattered, and it wasn't long before I became scared of what was going on. I decided to start using the medication again, but that this time I would slowly wean myself off of it. Once I did that, things somewhat returned to normal.

But my thoughts and emotions were out of whack.

51

A RETURN TO VANCOUVER

I felt cheated and sad. The car accident stole my dream of being a runway model. Even though I was 5'10", which was one or two inches shorter than what was ideal, I was very good at modelling. I could teach others the runway steps and I could coordinate entire shows. Before the accident, I would eat well and take care of my body by lifting weights to maintain my physique. My hygiene was impeccable. I always had a manicure, and my teeth were polished white. My eyebrows were manicured and shaped. I took great care of my skin, as well. I did whatever I needed to do to succeed.

But now I couldn't find that same individual within myself. In my head, that person had died in the car accident. I had never recovered that same sense of self. I felt like a failure. I felt like I had failed myself. Why couldn't I find that guy in myself? Why couldn't I see that passion? Was it because I was too scared to try because I was worried about what people would think? I kept telling myself, "You're too old, you don't have the same charisma as you once did. How do you think you can do it again?" I talked myself out of trying because I had a fear of rejection.

In spite of my thoughts, I had a friend who had never lost faith in who I was and who I could be again. His name was Allan. I remember one night, I was partying at a friend's house. Allan cornered me in an upstairs room, and he really let me have it.

He kept repeating, "Niall or Pepper, I am going to call you Niall, what are you doing? Why are you not modelling? Get the hell out of Saskatoon and go finish your dream."

I replied, "Allan, I am not that guy anymore."

He argued, "Yes, you are! You're scared, and you're a fucking pussy, man! You have to go back, man, 'cause if you don't, you will regret it for the rest of your life, brother."

I argued and tried to get my point across that I couldn't do it, but he wouldn't accept my answer and told me again that I needed to get out of Saskatoon and go back to Vancouver to at least try. He said that if I didn't, I was stupid and that he would still love me no matter what, but he would be very disappointed in the fact that I wouldn't even try. He also said that maybe I did change, but for the worse, because the guy he knew would get his ass back to Vancouver and follow the passion of his dream.

What Allan said echoed in my head for many days. Why was something I loved and was passionate about so hard to go back to? What was it that I was really scared of?

I thought about what Allan had said but there was a lot to consider. I was torn. On one hand, I was enjoying my job in telecommunication sales and had found my stride. My boss was also my friend and a great teacher about the business side of sales. But, Allan was telling me I could get back into the industry that I had always loved. The thought of working in fashion again and the possibilities and new opportunities that could come from it were enticing. But I also knew of all the party and drug dangers in fashion as well. I had a hard decision to make.

I summoned up my courage and I reached out to Noah in Vancouver.

Noah offered my job back. He said that things were still going well for him, but it didn't feel right without me because of our long history in the fashion industry. He offered me a chance to come back to Vancouver and get involved with his fashion brand again. With Allan's convincing words running through my head, I accepted

Noah's offer and flew back to Vancouver on November 8, 2015, to meet up with Noah for one more "kick at the can," as they say.

If it weren't for Allan, I would have never been able to get on that plane. The simple fact that a friend believed in me, even though I didn't believe in myself, is one of the greatest acts of kindness I can think of. If I hadn't taken Allan's advice, I always would have always wondered if I could have made it in fashion in Vancouver. I am grateful to have a friend like him.

When I landed at the Vancouver airport, Noah was there to greet me. I hadn't seen him since Edmonton.

The first thing he did was take my expensive watch off of my wrist and hand me one of the watches he designed. He left my watch on the ledge of a payphone. I thought this was kind of strange, but I went along with it to show my commitment to Noah. From all our years of working together, I knew how to play things cool with Noah, even if I wasn't cool. I won't kid you; I was choked. My watch was a nicer watch than the watch that Noah put on my wrist.

Noah was now taking care of his mom as she had developed dementia and needed help remembering to take her pills and so forth. I had met Noah's mom ten years earlier after her husband had died. When Noah and I arrived at his condo, his mom and I chatted and got caught up.

Noah and I went out on the town, but something was different this time around. There was no drugs and no boozing. Noah didn't party like he did back in the day. And that wasn't the biggest change in his life — he had gotten married to a twenty-four-year-old girl! Noah fought with her all the time; it was annoying, but I put up with it.

After I was all settled in and a week had gone by, Noah and I started to come up with a plan to get his fashion company back on the map and back into the fashion spotlight. We had been a big name, and it had been easy. Now, things were different. The root of fashion doesn't change; the basics were still the same — but now there was a lot more competition.

For Noah and I to pull this off, we had to start from scratch. This is where my new name August McQueen comes in. Noah chose the name as Alexander McQueen was a top British fashion designer and using McQueen's last name tied Noah to the staple in the fashion designer world. August was my birth month and a way to switch it up. Noah thought I needed a fresh name which sounded better than my given name. It is kind of weird but is perhaps smart in some strange way. I personally would have used the name Pepper Fox.

Noah asked my opinion on many things; some of my ideas he liked and used. He had designed some cool shirts and was making great progress. He also had some belt buckles and running shoes that he was working on. Setting up the company was going to take a while.

In the meantime, I helped Noah take care of his mom. I made sure she had her meds and would go for walks with her. I spent time with her so Noah could focus on his designs. Sometimes, I would take her to the gym; she was eighty-three, but she had a great drive, and for the most part, she enjoyed fitness. She enjoyed stretching and walking on the treadmill and rowing on the rowing machine. She is a special little lady; extremely witty and smart in many ways. She had a great sense of humor and a great laugh! I also walked Noah's dog, Reg, every morning and evening — it was cute and had a great personality and we hung out a lot.

But, almost immediately I noticed Noah's need to control everything. When I agreed to come, I told him that I had car payments. Noah told me that if I decided to come out to Vancouver, he would pay for my car payments and would make sure that all my bills were taken care of. He paid the first car payment but missed the next payments. I was not pleased. Eventually, my car was repossessed. My efforts to rebuild my credit were totally destroyed. I couldn't really do anything at the time because I was working for him, but I wasn't getting paid an average wage. I was right back where I had been years ago. I was technically trapped. I decided to put my head down and make the best of it. I had food and a roof over my head.

52

ASKING FOR FORGIVENESS

I found a nice gym near the waterfront. The view was fantastic! The membership was twenty-five dollars a month, which was an amazing price for the location. I made many friends there. I went to the gym two times a day, once at 5:00 a.m. when it opened, and once at night, when I would do abs and cardio. On top of my exercising, I was able to cook according to my fitness plan and do meal prep. I got into fantastic shape. I ate, slept, and dreamt about the gym. I started my days at 4:30 a.m. and was in the gym two times per day for six days a week. I was eating clean and exercising a fair amount. I don't call the amount I worked out excessive, but I was definitely on the cusp of excessiveness.

I directed my energy towards fitness, setting fitness modelling as a new goal. Fitness modeling focuses on body shape and being lean and muscular rather than the traditional runway physique. But I needed more than a new body, I needed a new train of thoughts, ideas, and new possibilities. When I was done with each workout, I wrote them down. I wrote idea after idea. I had many new projects running through my head, and I drowned myself in work. This fact sounds weird to me while I write it because I remember feeling that

I had never felt so driven. There were probably many things that contributed to my drive, and I had to work to understand it all on my own. Why was I doing all of this? Where did these ideas suddenly come from? What was I doing it for?

I started to attend church. At first, I was taking Noah's mom to a church; she liked to attend on Sundays. It was a Catholic church, which I didn't much care for, but I went so she could have her experience with God. The third time I attended this church, I sat at a pew and looked all around the building while admiring the stained glass and the architectural structure. My eyes were drawn to a corner, to the point where the beginning of a long, arched beam connected with another beam. I followed the other beam down and noticed a cable that was suspended up high as a support to an icon. The icon was Jesus hanging on the cross. Suddenly, I couldn't take my eyes off of the statue, and then a feeling came over me. Suddenly, I had a strong urge to pray, and I did.

I lifted my head, brought my hands together, crossed my fingers over one another and said: "O Lord, I know I haven't shown you my faith or lived by your word in a while. I have sinned many times. I have used drugs among my other sins. I am not perfect, nor do I pretend that I am, but I once asked you to be in my life. You entered my life, and it felt good. I remember being baptized. The feeling of coming out of the water was so refreshing, and I felt a huge weight lifted from my shoulders. I am sure that was your power. Lord, I feel lost in many ways, and I ask you to guide me and show me the direction I am supposed to go.

"Lord, I haven't always been the best brother, and I ask you to forgive me for neglecting my family, especially my sister, Nola. We have often not seen eye to eye on things, but I do try to be kind to her and, as you say in the Bible, to not cast the first stone and always turn the other cheek. I have always felt like the black sheep of the family due to the decisions I have made. Lord, I pray for my sister, Amber, and her husband Ken, and my nieces. I pray for my sister Denise, please keep her safe. May your spirit fill my extended family and friends' hearts.

"I pray for forgiveness from my parents if I have wronged them in any way. I pray, Lord, for my friend Paul who is struggling with the separation from his ex-wife. Give him, and his family, strength. I pray for my friend Rick who has a broken heart and still holds onto hate towards all women as a result. He is a great guy and deserves a change in heart; it would do him well.

"Lord, I pray to you knowing that you have worked many miracles in my life, some which I have recognized first hand. Pulling my body from that car accident, with hardly a scratch, was pretty impressive. Let's not try that one again. I thank you for keeping me out of harm's way, not only in the accident but also in some of the bad decisions I have made. You know what they are. Lord, let me feel your presence in my heart again. I ask you to forgive my past wrongs, and for sins, I will make in the weeks to come. Amen."

53

LACY

I started to make my own agenda. I set new goals in fitness modelling and networked on my own, away from what Noah was doing. I still helped him when he needed it, and when I was done with whatever he needed, I would get back on track with my goals. I planned a photoshoot with Alejandro, who was a photographer that Noah and I had talked to about shooting some of Noah's clothes. I booked a location, and we set a date and did the shoot. It was the first time that I had stepped in front of a camera since my car accident twelve years earlier. I knew that I had worked hard enough and planned it out properly. Noah wasn't too impressed that I was able to do the shoot but had not booked a time to shoot his clothing. He pulled me aside and let me know how upset he was. I told him that he had no concept for the shoot whatsoever. He said that it was my job to figure all that out. I didn't argue with Noah. I just said sorry and accepted the fact that he was disappointed in me.

I wanted to focus on a clean and healthy life. I was in desperate need of this. It was at this time that I finally reunited with an old friend from Edmonton, Lacy. We chatted a few times, and she told me that she wasn't the same girl that I had known back in the

Edmonton party days. Naturally, I was instantly intrigued. How had she grown? We finally met up after a few failed attempts. I remember being curious, excited, and happy when I went to see her. I hadn't seen her in eight years or so.

When I did see her, we walked toward one another and embraced. It was a wonderful feeling to see her. She had a big smile, and I am sure mine was just as big. We walked around downtown Vancouver, and she told me what she had been up to while living in Vancouver. She talked about some of her adventures and activities, but I was still waiting to hear about the big change. She had mentioned she was different and I wanted to know how.

She said she had different and better morals. We were only supposed to meet up for a coffee, but it wasn't long into our conversation before I felt I needed more time, and just coffee wasn't going to cut it. One of the things Lacy mentioned to me was that she wanted to eat cleaner and exercise. I offered to help her in any way with those things. I asked her if she would like to extend our meetup and head for some sushi. Lacy knew where all the good spots to eat were, and she suggested a place. It was an excellent meal, but that was nowhere close to the highlight of our time together. Eventually, she told me that she was attending a church downtown, and it was really good.

I always had some spirituality through my faith. When I arrived in Vancouver, I was trying to kick a long addiction to cocaine. I made a promise to myself that I would not go back to using it. Vancouver was my fresh start. Lacy and I sat and talked for hours over many pieces of sushi, cups of green tea, and a few glasses of water. At the end of our time, we shared a warm hug, and she suggested that maybe I should attend a church service with her as our next meet up. I definitely wasn't opposed to the idea.

As I walked home, many thoughts ran through my mind. One thought was how great it was to see my friend from years ago. I felt like we were just hanging out the week before and that no time had passed. It was a natural feeling, and I was surprised and thankful that there were no uncomfortable feelings that followed. I agreed to attend church with her and didn't see anything wrong with stepping back toward the church and Jesus. I saw that Lacy had been able to make positive changes in her life. She had a tough past and I just wanted to listen to her share how she had made her life-altering changes.

Attending church with Lacy was such an eye-opening experience. It was the first time that I enjoyed church as an adult. In the past, I attended churches where someone stood at the front of the church and basically blabbed. I didn't, usually, see the value of the message. That wasn't the case in this church at all. I found myself in tune and attentive to the pastor's words. He was an influential evangelical and Alpha pastor and was at the forefront of bringing in new Christians to have faith in Jesus. I was almost on the edge of my seat as I listened to the sermon. I often looked over in Lacy's direction and saw her smiling and giving praise by raising her arms in the air, which was new to me. I had never really witnessed so many people with their hands in the air giving praise to Jesus. When it came time to sing songs, I joined in and danced and sang, which I would rarely do in my past church experiences. Overall, it was a great experience, and I am thankful I went with Lacy.

Over time, Lacy and I made it a regular thing to attend an Alpha event at the Coastal church, one of the oldest churches in downtown Vancouver. The history of the building alone was exciting. I was hooked; not only was I working on my own troubled thoughts about cocaine, but I also enjoyed the opportunity to hang out with Lacy. I found myself thinking about how she was so different than other women I knew. She was happy and smiled and laughed a lot. She shared a lot in our conversations. She told me about where she had been and some of her own challenges. I was in complete awe and shocked by what she shared. She had a lot of strength. Where did she get her strength from?

It all became clear to me in one moment. She was full of the Holy Spirit. As we continued attending the Alpha course together, something began to brew in me. I found myself searching for what I saw in her. The Alpha course was eleven weeks long, and we attended many of the sessions together. Near the end of the course, we were invited to join the church on a trip to Cultus Lake for an event called the Holy Spirit Weekend.

Throughout the time we spent together, I always had to keep

my feelings for Lacy in check. My attraction to her was different from how it had been in the past. I am not sure how to explain these feelings, but I will give it my best shot. Back in the old days in Edmonton, I had a strong sexual attraction to Lacy. She was super-hot, and a lot of guys wanted her. While we attended Alpha together, I no longer had those feelings, and she was not the same girl that I had known years before. It was the strangest thing to lose that sense of lust toward her. I was attracted to who she was on the inside. It was as if our souls were flirting. I was cautious about showing my feelings, but I think she also felt the same way. I cannot speak for her, though, I am only assuming that she may have felt the same as me. There were times when we would lock eyes in conversation, and it was clear that there was a spark. Perhaps this spark was one that had stayed ignited throughout the years, or it could have been a new flame. Either way, I was confident that what I felt was true.

The time came to attend the Holy Spirit Weekend. I had access to an interesting vehicle which we ended up using to drive up to the lake. My friend owned a limo and allowed me to borrow it to bring people who needed a ride up to the lake. We arrived in style in this thirty-foot stretch limo; it was quite a hit with everyone who needed a ride. It was a fun little road trip. When we arrived, we settled in and dropped our bags off at our cabins.

There were group sessions to discuss various topics, and Lacy and I sat in the same groups. In between the sessions, we went for walks, talked, laughed, and reflected on what was going on and about the messages we heard in the groups. We jumped into the limo during one of the breaks and went for a drive. I asked Lacy if she wanted to drive, and she gladly took the opportunity since she found great joy in driving. We parked the limo in front of a gated off area, exited it, and walked down a road. It was a beautiful area to explore; there was vibrant, green moss covering the trunks of the trees. We continued to a stream and ventured down it to explore a bit more.

We walked on top of the rocks and took some pictures. The landscape was exquisite. We walked back up to the road and continued it; eventually, we came to a lake where there was a dock. The water was like glass, and we had a clear view of the mountains that surrounded us. I felt peaceful in this majestic scenery. It was the first time, in a long time, that I had the opportunity to spend some time in nature. We took a few more pictures, and then we headed back to the church in time for the service that was about to start. After the service, we walked over to another building for supper and enjoyed some great tasting food. Lacy and I are both fans of great tasting food, so we feasted.

The more time I spent with her, the more I felt something building up inside of me. I thought that a relationship with her was a long shot, but I couldn't keep my thoughts to myself much longer. During one of the breaks, I shared my feelings with Lacy. I said that I didn't understand what to do with them other than to express them to her. That is when the magic happened.

I was unsure and knew that it was possible that she may not feel the same way as I did. Thankfully, she expressed an interest in me as well. We discussed our past and present and what we thought the future might look like. In all cases, we talked about all the great feelings that we brought to one another. All our suppressed feelings were out in the open; she expressed to me that she felt the same. I felt a massive sense of relief because it could have gone in a totally different direction. I remember it was pleasant to hold her hand and just walk and talk. After the Holy Spirit Weekend, we returned back to the city and continued to go to the last few Alpha sessions to finish the course. It was in these last sessions that I was fortunate to experience a purity and calmness of mind. I would often go to sleep, and my mind would race, but during this time, I found pure thoughts. I no longer felt lust toward Lacy like I had in the past. I had a real heartfelt level of respect for her, and positive thoughts from my new found faith.

During this time with Lacy, I opened my heart to Jesus again. I allowed Him in to give me what I thought was absolutely necessary to finally defeat my addictions. At church one day, as I was being prayed upon, I raised my hands towards the heavens and truly spoke from my heart. I surrendered myself to God. I asked him to come into my heart and cleanse me once again of all my sins and free me from the temptations of drugs and all my devilish acts. I asked if he would make me new again. After all was said and done, this is what the aftermath from the prayer brought. I felt as if I had actually stepped out of my body and into another. I tried being fully conscious and very much in tune as to what was happening around me; I knew something significant had taken place. As I lowered my arms and opened my eyes, everything felt different to me. Again, I had that pure feeling, not perfect, but pure. I actually attempted more than once to instantly think of drugs and my long history with them, but I was unable to. Again, my mind was blown away by this unbelievable feeling that had come over me. I did not question this feeling and was filled with joy in my heart once again.

Shortly after this event, I attended church, and a woman encouraged me to ask to be filled with the Holy Spirit and I went to the front to be prayed for. The prayer only lasted about a minute. Now the only way I can explain what happened next is through a quote from Arnold Schwarzenegger: "Not many people understand what a pump is. It must be experienced to be understood. It is the greatest feeling that I get. I search for this pump because it means that my muscles will grow when I get it. I get a pump when the blood is running into my muscles. They become really tight with blood. Like the skin is going to explode any minute. It's like someone putting air in my muscles. It blows up. It feels fantastic."

Now, to anyone who has spent any time in the gym, they know what he is talking about. For those of you who haven't, I suggest you do some research because what happened to me next is simply unexplainable. I still have not come up with an explanation other than it was a physical manifestation of God, allowing me to physically see and feel his existence.

In the time it took me to stand, walk ten steps and get prayed upon for a minute, my entire body was pumped up. Now, I am just not talking about my biceps or triceps, which are fairly small muscle groups. I am talking about my entire body, starting from top to bottom. I will list what muscles were affected by this prayer of being topped up with the Holy Spirit. The areas were calves, hamstrings, quads, chest, back, biceps, triceps and even my forearms. The tightness was so intense that I had to shake my arms out as the blood-filled my muscles. I remember looking down and seeing my veins popped right out from my skin.

As a person who had spent countless hours in the gym, I know this just isn't possible. For me to reach such a level, I would need to do a full-body workout, and I would have to keep the muscles pumped that I started on as I move from body part to the next. This would take some time even if I was in the gym and had all the tools to even achieve the full body pump. I have tried to duplicate that same total pumped up feeling but I can't. I have tried flexing every muscle, all at once and have never even come close. I was filled with the Holy Spirit in the instant after the prayer was complete. I was pumped up!

It would be impossible for me to sit here and write or converse with a person and deny that God really does work inside to those who seek him and seek the truth. I feel very blessed that I have had these experiences. I have lived and seen both sides of good and evil. I have reaped the benefits of faith in God and been wrapped in the Devil's bad intentions. I will continue to finish the journey that has brought me to where I am today. As of right now, I am involved in a church where people raise their hands towards the heavens in praise to Jesus. I have seen people other than myself healed in the name of Jesus. I have seen others get full of the Holy Spirit, just as I did.

I witnessed a girl I had known from Saskatoon, Summer, be filled with the Holy Spirit. She started to speak in tongues as some laid praying hands on her. These are powerful events. I have watched people fall straight back not putting their arms out, and, boom, hit the floor and lay motionless while the service continued. They woke up as the service was ending and were not hurt, and they were completely filled full of the Holy Spirit. It is truly amazing stuff.

Over the next month, Lacy and I continued our relationship. We spent a lot of time, sharing new experiences. Lacy always knew of new spots to eat and got me to try new foods from different ethnicities. I tried Ethiopian, Mexican, Italian, and various others. I am not really the type to try new or different foods. Lacy will eat anything once, I think. She has a rebellious side to her in that she likes trying new things, which is a quality in her that I enjoy. She eventually had me try a mussel, and it tasted like dirt, but I finished it. It was totally gross, but I tried it just because it was great to try new things with Lacy. She brought things out in me. We always made an effort to avoid eating at the same place twice, which was fun in its own way.

We often walked her dogs, which gave us more time to chat and discuss future life goals and talk about our faith. It was a powerful time for me, and there was never a dull moment. Over the span of our time together, we also watched movies, enjoyed cuddles, and did little projects around her place.

Although things ended between us, I am grateful for my time with Lacy. Lacy encouraged me to do what I am passionate about, which is modelling. It is clear to me that God put us on the same path for reasons that I may not know at this time, but I am sure it will all become evident when the time is right.

Shortly after parting ways with Lacy, I became a born-again Christian. I summoned the strength to return to Saskatoon to be nearer to my family. Since returning to Saskatoon, I have been able to rebuild my relationship with all my family members—my mom, dad, and sisters. I have been able to rebuild myself and regain my confidence and feel proud of my moral choices. I have always been charismatic and outgoing on the outside, but my insides were torn to shreds. That has been rebuilt and is still under construction, but I am getting stronger.

I have allowed myself to feel vulnerable and share my struggles openly. I have told my dearest friends how much I appreciate their continued support and love. I have amazing friends. I have been able to not only beat — but crush — my twenty-three year-long addiction to cocaine. To those of you that may be struggling with addictions, make it easy on yourself, and turn to Jesus. That advice is the best I can give anyone, and that's free. No one told me, I had to find out the hardest way possible, through my own experiences.

CONCLUSION

In this book, I write of my darkest and most painful times in hopes that I can prevent others from making the same mistakes. Being sexually abused as a child resulted in trauma that created a life of destruction. I went from being an innocent carefree child to struggling with my self-worth, swarmed by inner demons.

I had a mission to prove to myself that I didn't like guys sexually. I looked to having sex with women as verification that I wasn't a boy who liked men. By the age of seventeen, I was driven to be with as many women as I could be. I believed that if I were with women all the time, it would counter the thoughts that perhaps I liked men. The number of women I was sexually active with grew into the double digits. With all the chaos going through my thoughts, this mission was how I coped and justified, in my head, that I didn't like men. My biggest fear was that I was gay.

I played all kinds of sports and was a jock in many ways. Still, these thoughts were always there, piercing my every thought. My abuse affected the way I looked at my male friends. It robbed me of my childhood innocence.

I wish I could find the words to explain the feeling, which still persists; I guess I could use words like disgusting, wrong, and disgraceful. Regardless of the word I attach to it, dealing with my feelings over my abuse has been the greatest challenge of my life.

For someone who hasn't experienced this kind of event, it might be easy for you to say, "Get over it already." Well, do you think that I, as a victim, don't want that? It is way harder than you may believe. I am sure that hundreds of thousands of people would agree with me in saying this. Now, in saying that, a person who has suffered sexual abuse can eventually come to terms with the facts and live a somewhat healthy life, but it will always come to mind from time to time. The emotion that I notice that comes to my thoughts is anger. Even in my twenties and thirties, I was affected by the actions that took place under the covers, in my room, and my own bed, as a child. I still have a gross feeling, even as I write this.

Coupled with the loss of my brother, Cyril, my sexual trauma cried out for a coping mechanism — and the one I chose was alcohol and drugs. But alcohol and drugs were only a band aid to the traumas and ultimately created a pathway of destruction. Only after facing the trauma head on did I find the strength in overcoming these tribulations. There were real dangers when it comes to drugs and alcohol; I understand now that I always had a choice, and I will have to live with the choices I made.

No one is responsible for your actions except yourself. Your friends will apply pressure on you to try cigarettes, weed, alcohol, and other drugs for various reasons. I want to leave you with a question: Are these people really your friends? Is a person, that you call a friend, who is pushing you to partake in drugs that may ultimately destroy you as a person, really a true friend? One that has your best interest at heart?

When I was a small boy, I wanted to become a police officer. A person who upholds the law and is there for the protection of the general public. Being in a two-decade-long cocaine addiction makes that type of goal tough to achieve. Within those twenty years, I cheated, became a thief, drug user, womanizer, and alcoholic. I had become the very person I wanted to help people against by being a police officer. Later in life, I had the chance to chase a new dream in the fashion world as a runway model. I made it farther than anyone I personally know, and I see that as a huge accomplishment. However, the drugs took over and I watched my dream once again fade into the shadows of the empty shell of my soul. No matter how hard I tried to do good in life, I would always get dragged down into the pit of nothingness. Now, there were other elements that contributed to the ending of my modelling career, but it was mainly my choice to use drugs as a crutch to my anger and disappointment that was my downfall.

The drugs always made me feel better, but only for a while. That great feeling quickly turned into loneliness, loss of relationships, anxiety, fear, anger, and a feeling of no self-worth. This is where I believe the real hurt comes from because you become a liar and a thief who harms others. You just don't care what you do anymore because you feel like you have nothing left to lose and that is where drugs lead you too. Drugs will take you to a place you don't want to be, and when you hit rock bottom, and you feel there is nowhere to turn, in most cases, there is only one last thought that will come to your mind. Suicide. What is your life worth? At the time you will think that your life's not worth living. You are mistaken.

You can always choose to do good, live a fun, fulfilled life, and do all the great things you dreamt of in life. You can find all the things that the drugs have stolen from you. You can rebuild your self-worth, you can find the joy in your heart that you think is gone.

A wise man once told me that you become who you are around the most. I have found this to be so powerful in overcoming my own demons in life. But it is more about identifying the negative people that surround you and remove them from your life. There is also the flip side of that coin, and it goes like this: If you surround yourself with happy, positive, energetic, goal-setting, successful, dreamers, it is only natural that you too will gain knowledge in becoming successful yourself. You can live a positive, fun, fulfilled life and gain your self-worth; again, the only thing stopping you is your decision. Decisions shape your life. That is a beautiful thing about life; you always have a choice.

After writing this book, two things have become clear to me. Number one, God really does have a plan for me. Two, I believe that in that plan I have earned the right to write this book, allowing me to reach out to you, the reader, in the hopes that I can help you through a difficult time. I want to help save the lives of those who feel they have nothing left in the tank and can't cope with life.

After being clean from drugs, with the power of giving my life back to Jesus, where there was once anger and hate, there is now happiness, joy, and love. From no self-worth to self-worth, I am living again and living with no fears. Looking at the world with a new set of eyes. I have been able to forgive my past and those who caused harm to me, along with the damage I created for myself.

If you hang onto the anger and choose not to forgive, you will carry that with you, and it will become heavy on your mind, body, and soul. My advice would be to let go of it all and look forward to your bright future. Your future is what you make it. Everyone has unique gifts to share with the world, and you always have something to offer. Remember that.

In my life, I have gone by many names. Douglas Bird, Niall Schofield, Pepper Fox, August McQueen. Regardless of the name I used, or the tag people called me, I am a man who fought a very hard battle with addictions and now stands victorious. I am a man who dreams again. I am a man who can look in the mirror and have the ability to love myself and others. I am a man who wants to help others and inspire them. I am a goal-driven machine. I am a man who will create positive change for those who seek it. I am a man who has rebuilt my core values, focusing on being the best I can be, not only to myself but to others. I am a man with strengths and desires, still chasing my dreams. I am a man who will not live in the past. I am a man who looks to the future with open arms, awaiting life's challenges while moving forward. Who am I? I am a survivor! I am God's creation.

.

www.ingramcontent.com/pod-product-compliance
Lightning Source LLC
Chambersburg PA
CBHW071733120626

46550CB00002B/511